PRO
FOOTBALL HEROES
OF TODAY

Exciting illustrated profiles of 22 stars who excel at every football skill—quarterbacks, runners, pass receivers, linemen, linebackers, pass defenders. Every fan will find a favorite in this line-up of championship players.

PRO FOOTBALL

illustrated with photographs

HEROES OF TODAY

BY BERRY STAINBACK

Random House · New York

PHOTOGRAPH CREDITS: John Biever, 12, 38, 54, 73, 146; Vernon Biever, 11, 31, 33, 34, 35, 36, 41, 43, 55, 67, 85, 102, 106, 141; Dick Darcey—Camera 5, 3 (top), 133, 134; Malcolm Emmons, endpapers, 2 (bottom left), 3 (bottom), 6, 24, 29, 30, 40, 42, 45, 46, 48, 52, 57, 61, 63, 64, 65, 69, 75, 76, 91, 94, 98, 109, 110, 115, 123, 129, 138, 139; Philadelphia Eagles, 22, 23; Ken Regan—Camera 5, 2 (bottom right), 8, 97; Fred Roe, 47, 66, 79, 93; Al Satterwhite—Camera 5, 58, 59, 70–71; Dan Sterbling—Camera 5, 5, 144; United Press International, 1, 2 (top), 14, 15, 16, 21, 27, 28, 49, 51, 53, 77, 80, 84, 86, 89, 95, 101, 104, 107, 108, 112, 116, 121, 126, 127, 128, 130, 131, 135 137, 144, 148; Wide World Photos, 18, 82, 88, 99, 117, 118, 119, 122, 125, 143.

COVER: SPORTS ILLUSTRATED photos by Walter Iooss, Jr. (top left, bottom left), Neil Leifer (top right, bottom right), © Time Inc.

Library of Congress Cataloging in Publication Data
Stainback, Berry. Pro football heroes of today. (Landmark giant)
SUMMARY: Profiles the lives of twenty-two champion football players including Joe Namath, Dick Butkus, Otis Taylor, and Larry Brown. 1. Football—Biography—Juvenile literature. [1. Football—Biography] I. Title. GV939.A1S73 1973 796.33′2′0922 [B] [920] ISBN 0-394-82629-9 73-4434 ISBN 0-394-92629-3 (lib. ed.)

For Rita

Contents

Introduction

You may remember the game-tying catch Kansas City's Otis Taylor made against the Washington Redskins in 1971. It was a Monday night game on national television. Taylor raced into the end zone, made his cut, then leaped as quarterback Len Dawson's pass descended into the corner. Redskin cornerback Pat Fischer leaped right along with Taylor and his body pinned Otis's left arm to his side.

There was no way Taylor could pull in that ball. Yet he reached up instinctively with his right arm. The ball landed in his large right hand, and his fingers wrapped around the pebbled leather and held it. Touchdown! It was some kind of magic trick, I thought. Then I learned that Otis Taylor actually *practiced* one-handed catches just so he would be prepared for such situations.

There are, of course, "tricks" of the trade in every position in pro football. You'll read about many of them in this book: everything from the unusual ball-carrying style of offensive halfback Larry Brown to the super-aggressive pass-blocking style of offensive tackle Bob Brown.

Stars at nearly every football position are covered here—quarterbacks, receivers, running backs, linebackers, pass defenders, and offensive and defensive linemen. There are other leading football heroes that might have been included, but there was room for only 22. I'm sorry to say that even using two hands I found no magic trick to make room for everyone. I'm sure, though, that there won't be any quarrels with the superb players who have been included. Their magic speaks for itself.

BERRY STAINBACK

PRO
FOOTBALL HEROES
OF TODAY

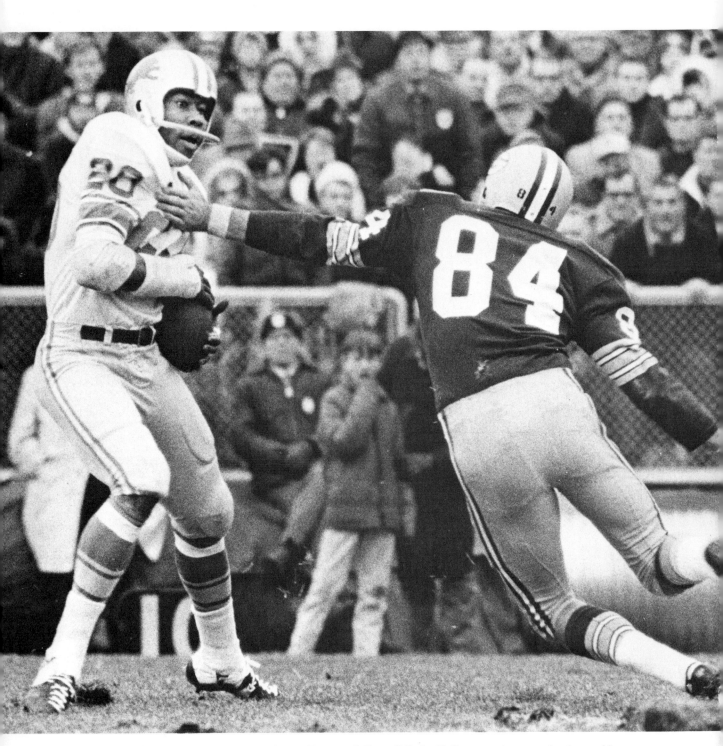

Lem Barney intercepts against Green Bay, and Carroll Dale (84) comes in to make the tackle.

Lem Barney

The rookie left cornerback for the Detroit Lions smiled. It was September 1967. Lem Barney was going into his first pro game, yet he didn't seem worried at all. A coach reminded him to be on his toes. The opposing quarterback, Bart Starr of the Green Bay Packers, would be testing the rookie to see if he could do his job. A cornerback must defend against passes, and Starr was one of the best passers of the day. As he ran onto the field for the first time in the NFL, Lem Barney was still smiling. He was confident of his ability.

Bart Starr wasted no time in testing Barney. The Packers had the ball on their 18-yard line. Starr called a play that would send two receivers into Barney's territory. Boyd Dowler would run down the right sideline, and Barney would have to cover him. Then halfback Elijah Pitts would come out of the backfield into the area Barney had left wide open.

Starr looked over the defense and began calling signals. The ball was snapped, and Dowler ran his sideline pattern. Barney picked him up for about ten yards. Somehow the rookie read the play, realizing Pitts was the primary receiver, so he left Dowler to another Lion defender and hurried back to cover Elijah Pitts. Starr threw the ball low and short to Pitts, hoping that Pitts could turn and come back for it. If he couldn't, the pass would probably go incomplete—it seemed too low for anyone to intercept. But Starr didn't know how quick and agile Barney was.

Lem saw the pass as he approached Pitts, and he dove for the ball, his body sailing about eight yards in the air, his arms outstretched. Just as his hands scraped the field, the ball settled in them. Barney slid on his belly, then popped up onto his feet and ran the ball into the end zone 24 yards away. He had intercepted the very first pass thrown his way in the NFL and returned it for a touchdown.

"I didn't even know I was running in the right direction," said Barney, laughing in the locker room afterward. "I started to run and hoped I was going the way I was supposed to."

That first season Barney led the league with eleven interceptions. He returned three of them for touchdowns, which tied a league record. In addition, he returned kickoffs, missed field-goal attempts and punts for touchdowns.

"I think Lem Barney is the greatest athlete the Lions will *ever* have," said veteran defensive tackle Alex Karras. "He can do more things than any ball player that ever played with the Lions."

Barney was named Defensive Rookie of the Year after the 1967 season. "I wish I had two others just like him," said his coach, Joe Schmidt. "I could play one next to him on defense, and I'd use the other on offense. But since I've only got one Barney, he'll stay at the corner. The best athletes on your team play there. You can't possibly hide at cornerback. The receivers come at you one-on-one, and you just can't hide. You either make the play or you don't—it's that simple. Barney makes the play because of his speed, his quickness, his reactions and his senses."

Even when he missed the interception, Barney sometimes made the big play. In a game against the Jets, Lem just missed intercepting a Joe Namath pass. Star receiver Don Maynard caught the ball and seemed to be headed for a touchdown. But Barney spun around, reached out and popped the ball out of Maynard's arm. He grabbed the ball in midair, turned again and headed for the other goal line.

Dallas coach Tom Landry saw this play on film when his team was preparing to play the Lions. "Barney's dangerous even after you catch the ball," said Landry. "You can beat him, and he'll still beat you."

Landry prepared well for the Lions, and his Cowboys won, 59–13. They completed 19 passes, but not a single one was thrown in Lem Barney's area.

Barney himself was a quarterback at 33rd Avenue High School, a black school in Gulfport, Mississippi. He was a better runner than passer, and college coaches weren't very interested in his talents.

"First of all, I didn't want to go to college," Lem recalled. "But my mother, being as persistent as she is, persuaded me to try it for one year. So I went to Jackson State [a predominantly black school in Jackson, Mississippi]. After getting there and seeing the different brand of sports and the caliber of people, I accepted the challenge."

Barney played very little as a quarterback on the freshman team. He decided that the position for him was cornerback and asked the coach to switch him. He made the All-Conference team at cornerback three straight years. He also set a school record by intercepting 26 passes in those three varsity seasons.

The Lions were so impressed they made Barney their second draft choice. Although he was a defensive back from a small college, Lem was picked by the Lions as one of the top 20 players in the country.

Cornerback Barney—"The best athletes on your team play there," said his coach.

Kick-returner Barney gains 25 yards against the Los Angeles Rams in a 1970 game.

Coach Joe Schmidt was asked about Barney's chances of starting right away. "They're pretty darn slight," said Joe. "That's one of the most difficult spots in football. It takes time to learn it, a little longer than the other positions. There aren't too many who come in their first year and play the corner."

Schmidt changed his mind about Barney in the first scrimmage at training camp. Lem was covering veteran Lion receiver Gail Cogdill. Cogdill drove straight downfield at Barney, then made a sharp cut to the center of the field. As he reached for the ball, Lem knocked it away. Cogdill gave the rookie a dirty look and went back to the huddle. On the next pass play Cogdill again drove straight at Barney, faked to the inside, then stopped dead, spinning around for the chest-high pass that was spiraling at him. Lem did not take the fake. He leaped up, reached over Cogdill's shoulder with one hand—and intercepted the ball!

The 6-foot, 185-pound youngster had a flair and a style all his own right from the beginning. In 1968 he returned a blocked field goal 77 yards to beat the Redskins, 21–20. Lem had caught the ball in the air at the Lion's 23-yard line. He made a couple of tricky moves to slice through a swarm of Redskins, then turned on the speed down the sideline. At the Washington 30 he turned and saw four big Redskins some ten yards behind. Lem waved to them. Then he began to slow down. As he drew closer to the end zone, the four slower men were catching up. They were within two yards of him when he crossed the goal line. After this bit of dramatics, his teammates called him "Stroller," for the easy way he had strolled into the end zone.

"I like to conserve my energy," he

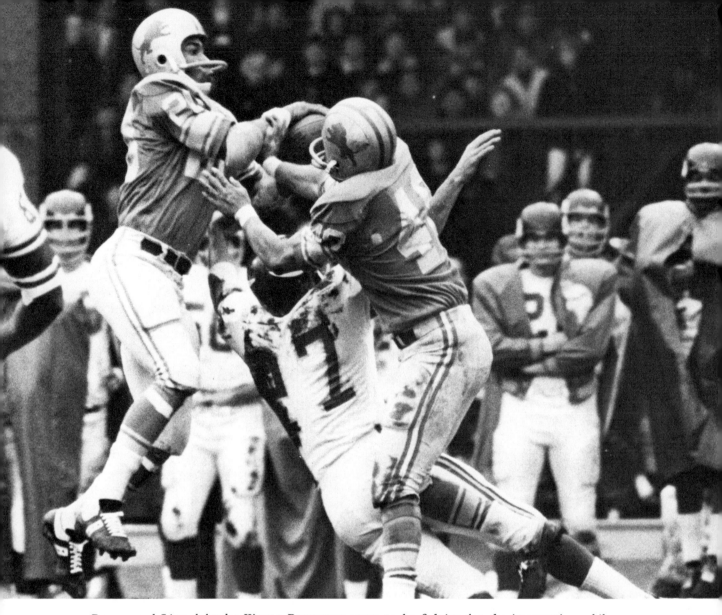

Barney and Lion defender Wayne Rasmussen seem to be fighting for the interception while Minnesota's Bob Grim, the intended receiver, falls by the wayside.

said later, laughing. "I wasn't showboating. I slowed down because I wanted to make sure the TV cameraman had me all the way."

In the same game, Barney took another dramatic "stroll." The Lions' regular punter had been sidelined, and Lem was doing the punting. He came in in a punting situation, took the snap, tucked the ball under his arm and ran for a first down. Even the Lions hadn't expected that.

"I saw Schmidt scratching his head and figured that must be the sign to run," said Barney, again laughing.

"He's unbelievable," said Schmidt. "No matter what he's asked to do, he does it in spectacular fashion."

One of Lem's most spectacular performances was in the last regular game of 1970. The Lions had to defeat the Packers if they were to qualify for the playoffs. The Detroit offense was having trouble, but at the half the Lions had a 3–0 lead. Then Barney ran back the second-half kickoff 74 yards. The Lions were only able to score a field goal, but that gave them a 6–0 lead. Lem gave the offense another chance by returning a punt 65 yards. Quarterback Greg Landry followed this with a touchdown pass, and Detroit was ahead 13–0.

Barney still wasn't satisfied. He intercepted a Bart Starr pass, started up one sideline, cut all the way across the field, faked left, right, left, then swerved back across the field into the corner of the end zone. Although he was credited with a 49-yard touchdown run, Lem had actually traveled more than 100 yards. In a game in which the combined total offense for both teams was 286 yards, Barney accounted for 233 yards himself.

"I had to do something to justify the kind of year I've had," said Barney in the locker room after that game. He went on to explain that in 1970 he hadn't had a bad season, but he had had a couple of bad afternoons.

Lem definitely had not played up to his All-Pro standards of the previous three years. There were several reasons. An injured ankle had bothered him through several games and kept him from cutting sharply. He had also been involved in stormy salary negotiations with the Lions. At a time when Joe Namath and other superstars were getting huge contracts, Barney was earning only $16,000 per year after three great seasons. The bitter contract dispute he had to go through with the Lions affected his play.

Barney's other problem in 1970 was that he gambled too much going for interceptions. When he gambled and lost, the receiver would often catch the ball and go for a touchdown. Lem wanted

to break the NFL record of 14 interceptions in a season set by Night Train Lane in the 1950s. But going after the record was costly for the Lions.

"I love to gamble," said Lem, going into the 1971 season. "It's a matter of instinct. A little voice tells you 'now,' and you go. But you have to temper that feeling. This year I plan to settle down to playing basic, sound defensive football."

He did settle down, and the result was that quarterbacks regarded Barney as so dangerous that they virtually stopped throwing in his area. So his interception totals fell off. But his gambling style of play did not completely disappear on those rare occasions when passers dared to test him.

As his wife Martha once said, "Lem likes challenges. He likes the ball to come in his direction. He thinks he has just as much chance to get it as the receiver."

"He lays in the bushes," said Lion safetyman Mike Weger, who played the left side behind Barney. "Lem will run at three-quarter speed, letting his man get two or three steps ahead of him. If this fools the quarterback—and it often does—he throws a pass. Then Lem, who has this incredible burst of speed, bursts in there for the interception."

Perhaps the best description of Lem Barney came from his long-time roommate and best friend on the Lions, fullback Mel Farr. "If ever a man was made to be a cornerback, Lem is it," said Farr. "He's not overly fast, but he's quick—the quickest one in the game—and he's smart. He plays the position like no one else. Maybe like no one else ever will."

17

Bill Bradley

In 1971, his first season as a regular with the Philadelphia Eagles, free safety Bill Bradley intercepted eleven passes and was named to the All-Pro team.

When the rest of the Eagles assembled at training camp the following year, Bradley had not yet signed a contract to play. Instead of driving to the Eagles'

Philadelphia's defensive back and kick-returner, free spirit Bill Bradley.

training camp, he drove to a beach town in New Jersey and settled down to enjoy himself. He drove a blue Volkswagen bus with a name lettered on its side—"Cottonmouth Blues Wagon." Cottonmouth is a Texas expression that means thirsty.

When asked what he would do if he didn't play football, the unconventional Bradley said, "I hope to get a vending license and sell sandwiches and drinks on the practice field at the Eagles' training camp."

Bradley didn't need a vending license. The Eagles finally offered him a new three-year contract for a reported $140,000—about what he had asked for weeks earlier. The self-assured young man was willing to hold out until he was paid what he felt he was worth. And if he couldn't earn what he was worth playing football, he wouldn't mind coming to camp to sell sandwiches. Obviously Bill Bradley was not only a free safety, he was a free spirit.

He was also an enormously talented athlete. Growing up in Palestine, Texas, Bill starred in all sports. When he finished high school, the Detroit Tigers offered him a $50,000 contract to play shortstop. "I like football better," said Bradley. "Besides, I wanted to go to college."

A sensation as a high school quarterback, he accepted a football scholarship to the University of Texas. Before reporting to the university team, he played in an annual all-star game between Texas and Pennsylvania high school seniors. In it he passed for two touchdowns and ran for another. On defense he intercepted three passes as the Texas All-Stars won, 26–10. After the game,

Doak Walker, a coach of the All-Stars and a former Detroit Lion star, said, "I'll just bet when Bradley takes off that uniform, there'll be a big red S on his chest—just like Superman."

When Bradley reported to the University of Texas team, the publicity director, Jones Ramsey, gave him a nickname: "Super Bill." Soon even his teammates were using it.

"I sat down with them and we talked about it," said Bill. "I was afraid they'd resent it. But I said to them, 'Heck, you guys are my friends—you can just call me Soup.' They laughed, and that broke the pressure."

Bradley had a great year with the freshman team and went into his sophomore year with one of the biggest publicity build-ups ever witnessed in the Southwest Conference. He was an all-league player before he had played in his first varsity game, according to the newspapers. *Playboy* Magazine predicted he would be the best sophomore in the country, and Bill stepped right in as the Longhorns' starting quarterback. But he hurt his knee in the season's second game, and under his leadership Texas won only six games and lost four.

"I played with the leg all taped up," Bradley recalled. "But I didn't have a very good year. Ol' Super Bill was kind of a disappointment."

The bad knee wobbled under Bradley through his junior year, too, and Texas again had a 6–4 record. Then Bradley had some cartilage and part of his kneecap removed by surgery. He went into his senior year in perfect physical condition. But after Texas lost its first two games, it was apparent that Bill simply did not pass well enough to play quarter-

19

back. Coach Darrell Royal called him to his office.

"He told me James Street would play quarterback the rest of the way," said Bill. "He'd decided to make me a wide receiver. I was really upset. Coach Royal later said the way I left his office, he didn't think I'd ever come back."

But Bradley went to his room and pushed aside his anger. That afternoon he showed up at practice and lined up with the receivers.

"There were a lot of people at practice and I knew why," said Bill. "They wanted to see how I'd act. I nudged the guy who was lined up next to me. 'Watch this,' I said, and I untied the string holding up my sweat pants.

"So when I ran out for my first pass, my pants fell right down to my ankles. I landed on my face. When I looked around, coach Royal was laughing so hard he threw his clipboard up in the air. Everyone roared. I knew I had to do something to break the tension. The other guys looked up to me for taking the switch the way I did."

Later Bradley was shifted again, this time to deep safety on defense. He had finally found his spot. On Thanksgiving day Texas played arch-rival Texas A & M and Bill intercepted four passes. Texas won its last seven games, including the Cotton Bowl.

Bradley was an important factor in the abrupt turnaround in Texas' fortunes. As a defensive back, he revealed a tremendous instinct for the ball, great quickness and a shifty running style that allowed him to pick up very large chunks of yardage in returning interceptions and kicks. And he had still another

asset that recommended him to pro scouts—he was a left-footed punter who put a reverse spin on the ball that made it hard for opponents to field.

In 1969 the Philadelphia Eagles drafted him on the third round, and he spent most of the year punting and running back punts and kickoffs. He was also a tackler on the defensive special teams. Perhaps his best game as a rookie was against the Cowboys in Dallas. Bradley punted seven times for a 44.7-yard average, and those punts were returned for a mere 14 yards. Bill also ran back four Cowboy punts for a total of 65 yards and returned two kickoffs for 36 yards. In addition, he filled in for regular free safety Joe Scarpati and picked off a Roger Staubach pass, carrying it 56 yards for a touchdown. As he crossed the goal line, Bill raised the ball over his head in celebration. Then Cowboy end Bob Hayes smacked into him from behind, not realizing Bradley was in the end zone. Bill notified him of that fact by turning and bouncing the ball off Hays' helmet.

"This is home to me, and if I did anything which the fans thought deserved to be booed, I'm sorry," Bill said as he dressed after the game. "I wasn't mad." He smiled. "I just did it deliberately."

At season's end Joe Scarpati was traded, clearing the way for Bradley to take over at free safety in 1970. But in the opening exhibition game he tore up a knee trying to make a tackle. The knee was operated on the next day, and just six weeks later Bill was back working out with the Eagles. Again he injured the knee. Bill continued to punt for the Eagles because they had no one

As a sophomore at the University of Texas, quarterback Bradley runs with the ball against Southern California. He is being tackled by Tim Rossovich, later Bradley's teammate with the Eagles.

else; but the snap had gone out of his knee, and he averaged only 36.8 yards per kick.

"Mr. Bradley's average was 36.8 yards more than should have been expected of him," declared Eagle doctor James Nixon after he performed a second operation on Bill's knee. His injury "might well have prevented *any* performance in an average individual," said the doctor.

Bill went through a tough rehabilitation program from January till May, then returned to Philadelphia to have his progress checked. He was depressed. "I've been here two years and haven't done a thing," he said. "I just can't believe that I'm washed up. But this knee

business has been the most frustrating thing in my life."

Bill and a friend then went off and hitchhiked through Europe for a month. But Bradley continued to work on his knee, running three miles every day. He rejoined the team in time for the opening of training camp, and quickly won the free safety job. His knee was fine, but the Eagles weren't. They lost the first five games of the 1971 season, and this didn't sit well with Bill, who was a fiery competitor. He was playing a very tough defense, yet his team was losing and he kept getting fined for blowing up.

One of his early fines came in a game against Denver when he intercepted a pass and ran it back for a touchdown.

The trouble was that he didn't stop in the end zone. Bill kept running right to the stands, and threw the ball to a fat man in the first row who he thought would like to have it. The league levies an automatic $100 fine on players who toss balls into the stands, but Bill didn't care. The interception had saved an Eagle victory.

Bradley's frustration over losing also cost him several penalties. Against the Cowboys he made a late tackle on tight end Mike Ditka, and looked as if he was trying to tear Mike's head off.

"It was over-emotion," Bill admitted later. "He wasn't down and I wanted to make sure he did go down. There's nothing between Mike and me. It just happened that I was covering him a couple of times earlier and we were jaw-boning [challenging or insulting each other] a lot. I'm pretty sure that's the

way it's going to be until we start winning."

"None of it bothered me," said Ditka, who had himself played with the losing Eagles in other years. "Let him try to rip my head off. Look, I've been in his position—down—and you don't have anything to do to pick yourself up. So you blow your top and start hitting people."

Probably the most amazing thing was that, for all Bradley's emotionalism, he continued to play exceptional football week after week, and his interception totals kept growing. His tenth interception, against Detroit, showed just how sly a safetyman Bill had become as the Eagles upset the Lions 23–20 and knocked them out of playoff contention.

The Lions were driving for what would have been the winning touchdown, and quarterback Greg Landry

Bradley intercepts a pass thrown by New England's Jim Plunkett in 1972.

called what seemed to be the perfect play to tie up Bradley and produce a scoring pass. He sent fullback Steve Owens across the middle to occupy Bill, then sent tight end Charley Sanders in behind Bradley against a lone corner-back. Bradley sensed the play, dropped off Owens, zipped back in front of Sanders and intercepted in the end zone. He ran the ball back 51 yards to preserve the Eagle victory.

"Landry may have been surprised," said Eagle coach Jim Carr, "but I wasn't. One of Bill's biggest assets is his knack of being around the ball, wherever the action is."

The following week Bradley intercepted his eleventh pass of the 1971 season to lead the league. His 248 yards in returns set an all-time Eagle record. Bill picked up right where he'd left off in 1972 by again leading the NFL in interceptions, picking off a total of nine passes.

In game number four, against Washington, he made perhaps the most spectacular interception of his career. Redskin quarterback Sonny Jurgensen called one of his favorite play-action passes—faking a running play, then quickly flipping to tight end Jerry Smith in the corner of the end zone. Certainly Smith, who had blocked briefly and then slipped across the goal line, was wide open when Jurgensen released his pass. But suddenly Bradley darted in front of him, raised an arm and caught the ball one-handed.

"I really like that one," Bradley said with a smile after the game. "It looked pretty, one-handed and all."

And it sure beat selling sandwiches from his "Cottonmouth Blues Wagon," as Bradley would be the first to admit.

As a wall of Eagle blockers forms, Bradley sets out to return a kick.

Terry Bradshaw

Terry Bradshaw was without doubt the most highly regarded small-college quarterback ever to join the pros. An outstanding passer at Woodlawn High School in Shreveport, Louisiana, he chose to accept a scholarship to little Louisiana Tech. There he broke all the school's passing records and dominated the college division All-America teams for three years in a row.

A 6-foot-3, 218-pounder, he became known as the man with the Golden Arm. His legs were at least silvery, and he had the speed of most NFL running backs. Pro scouts said he could step right in and be an NFL star as a rookie—that Bradshaw had even more potential than Joe Namath had in his first season.

Bradshaw finished his college career in 1969, a year in which the Pittsburgh Steelers won only one game. This gave them the first choice in the NFL draft. Naturally, the Steelers picked Bradshaw, who read all the nice things that had been written about him and believed the pro scouts were right. Bradshaw—who in 1972 would indeed lead the Steelers to their first NFL title ever—figured he would step in and tear up the pro league as a rookie.

Steeler coach Chuck Noll was not as optimistic as the easygoing, outgoing, enthusiastic Bradshaw. Noll's quarterback in 1969 had been Terry Hanratty, an All-America from Notre Dame. Hanratty had not been a raving success, but he'd had a great college record at a major school and had worked in Noll's system for a year. Noll said Bradshaw would have to win the job as number one quarterback, and that it would undoubtedly take some time.

It took exactly 30 minutes. In the first exhibition game in 1970, Bradshaw started the second half with the Steelers trailing the Miami Dolphins 13–0. Though the Steelers lost 16–10, Bradshaw's passing and leadership were so impressive that he earned a start in the next preseason game against the powerful Minnesota Vikings. This time Bradshaw produced a victory. The Steelers were the youngest team in the league. Bradshaw and all three of his starting receivers were rookies. Yet they finished the exhibition season with wins over the New York Giants, the Boston Patriots and the Oakland Raiders.

Bradshaw's passing statistics were not exceptional. But he was a leader, and he could move the team. He conveyed his great enthusiasm and confidence to his teammates, much as Bobby Layne had in quarterbacking Steeler teams years ago.

"I was on cloud nine," Bradshaw said. "Everything was great. As a quarterback, I didn't have a great preseason. But we won, the team did. That was the important thing. The guys played great defense, we had a solid running attack and everybody felt this was going to be our year."

Then the Steelers opened the season against the Houston Oilers at Pittsburgh's beautiful new Three Rivers Stadium. The stands were packed. The game was nationally televised. And big, blond-haired, Golden Armed super-rookie Terry Bradshaw went out to show what he could do in regular-season competition. Now the games counted in the standings, and opposing teams were no longer experimenting with untried players.

The Oilers chewed Bradshaw up. The

Steelers as a team had too many breakdowns, particularly in blocking for Bradshaw. But he obviously had trouble reading defenses and, despite several scrambles for good gains, ran out of the passing pocket too often. He completed four of 16 passes. Three others were dropped by his inexperienced receivers.

A couple of times Terry's Golden Arm deserted him. On one play, wide receiver Ron Shanklin raced deep down the middle and outdistanced the Oiler defenders. Bradshaw dropped back quickly, spotted him, set, stepped and threw. The ball slipped off his hand. Even with the slip, the ball wobbled 55 yards in the air, and Shanklin managed to come back to catch it. "If he didn't have to come back for it, he'd have scored easily," said Bradshaw.

But the Golden Arm wasn't succeeding. He was replaced by Hanratty late in the third quarter. "The benching put a lump in my throat," he admitted later, "but I wasn't moving the team. The guys were open. I just wasn't hitting them."

Bradshaw was so dejected as he left the field that when he was asked to appear on the postgame radio show, he said, "Not today. I don't feel up to it." However, Terry gave some indication of what kind of man he was a few minutes later. He showed up at the radio booth. "I've been thinking about that interview," he said. "I'll go on if you still want me. I went on when we won. I guess I have to learn to take the bitter with the sweet."

He got more of the bitter than the sweet in his rookie season. He was tackled for safeties in each of the first three games and didn't complete a touch-

down pass until game five. During the seventh game he was benched. Terry Hanratty went in and led the Steelers to a 21–10 win over Cincinnati. That was probably the most discouraging night of Bradshaw's life. And he didn't know how to handle the humiliation and disappointment. He popped off to the press in the locker room.

"I don't want to play second-fiddle to Hanratty," he said. "I don't mind playing behind somebody older, somebody ready to retire, but I surely won't play behind someone my age. If the Steelers are going to do that, they better trade me."

Hanratty was dressing right beside him and heard the whole thing. The comments didn't please the rest of the Steelers or coach Noll, who snapped, "Bradshaw has a lot of growing up to do—both on the field and off it."

Bradshaw had not meant what he said in that moment of total frustration, and he later apologized to Hanratty. But he stumbled through the remainder of the season. The more mistakes he made, the more he forced his passes into crowds and generally fouled up. His confidence steadily diminished. He finished with the lowest completion percentage in the league (38.1 percent) and had 24 passes intercepted.

"By the time the season ended I just wanted to go home and get football out of my mind," he confessed. "But by February, I was mentally ready and anxious for the new season to start. I knew I had to beat out Hanratty, and I was going to make doggone sure I was in the right frame of mind. I wouldn't want to go through another year like that first year—but the experience was

Out of action with an injury, Bradshaw keeps warm on the sidelines during the 1971 season.

priceless. I faced everything a young man can face: a bad press, caused by me; and a bad performance, also all my fault."

There was a dramatic change both in the attitude and performance of Terry Bradshaw during his second season. The Steelers had hired Babe Parilli to coach the Steeler passers. Parilli was a former NFL quarterback himself and had played for such outstanding quarterback coaches as Bear Bryant, Vince Lombardi, Paul Brown and Weeb Ewbank. Parilli worked hour after hour with Bradshaw, teaching him how to rec-

ognize defenses at the line of scrimmage, teaching him how to take a little velocity off his passes. The coaching soon showed in Bradshaw's improved performance.

"He threw much too hard a year ago," Parilli said during the 1971 season. "That's why he had so many interceptions. The ball would bounce off a receiver's shoulder into the arms of a defensive back. He's throwing it softer now, laying it in there."

"Babe and I are awfully close," said Bradshaw. "He talks my language and I talk his. I can tell him anything on my mind and he understands it and he'll react. I'll tell you the big thing he does, though. He doesn't let me get down. I'm my own worst critic, but Babe doesn't let me get down on myself."

The most important thing Bradshaw had to learn was to stay cool, to keep his poise in the face of heavy pressure from defensive lines. In his first season he had done everything in a rush. He hurried his passes, he hurried his hand-offs on running plays, he hurried his fakes. He concentrated all through the '71 season on settling down and giving

the play a chance to develop before getting rid of the ball.

"I'm trying to sit in the pocket and act cool," he said then. "When you do this, you can read your keys. If your number one receiver is covered, you have to look for your number two. Usually he's open. If he's not, you're gonna be tackled or you have to sprint out."

An excellent runner, Bradshaw sprinted out very well. But he learned a lesson there in 1971, too. When he joined the Steelers he said he saw no point in running out of bounds if he

A fine runner as well as a passer, Bradshaw carries the ball over the goal himself in a 1971 game.

scrambled deep into the secondary. Defensive backs weighed a good deal less than Terry's 220 pounds, so he figured he could hold his own. But he soon realized that if four or five men came up to tackle him, their size wouldn't make much difference.

He learned that lesson in a game against Cincinnati. Darting out of the pocket, Terry burst right up the middle, faked out a big tackle, then dodged a linebacker. But another tackle, Dave Chomyszak, hustled over and grabbed him. Instead of going right down, Bradshaw fought for extra yardage, which was always his habit when hit. But when Chomyszak finally wrestled him to the ground, middle linebacker Bill Bergey cracked Bradshaw in the jaw with a forearm.

"I got him right in the choppers!" yelled Bergey.

Bradshaw was helped off the field for a time till his head stopped ringing. After the game he decided, "I guess I better start running out of bounds from now on."

It was one of many lessons Terry Bradshaw learned the hard way. But he also made a lot of progress during his second year as a pro. Where as a rookie he had completed only 83 of 218 passes, as a sophomore he hit on 203 of 373 passes for 2,259 yards and 13 touchdowns. He also ran for five touchdowns himself.

"He's improving with every game," said Babe Parilli. "His poise is now exceptional, and he can hurt you both passing and running. Either way, he comes up with the big play, and that's the sure sign of a winner."

Bradshaw helped make Pittsburgh a big winner in 1972. He was ably supported by a superb all-round defense, a fine offensive line and a sensational rookie running back, Franco Harris. But it was Terry Bradshaw who led this suddenly efficient young machine. The Steelers, who finished 5–9 in 1970 and 6–8 in '71, won 11 of 14 regular season games in '72 to win the AFC's Central Division title, then defeated Oakland in the playoffs.

They might well have defeated Miami in the AFC championship game, too, if Bradshaw had been healthy. Terry

Bradshaw pivots in the backfield as his blockers protect him.

Golden Arm Bradshaw took the Steelers into the playoffs in 1972 — with the help of rookie running back Franco Harris, who carries the ball on this play.

spent the week before that game in the hospital with the flu. Early in the game he marched the Steelers to a touchdown against the Dolphins but was knocked out on the scoring play. By the time he was clear-headed enough to return, there were only seven minutes left and the Dolphins had built up a 21–10 lead.

Terry promptly completed four passes in a row for 72 yards and a touchdown to cut the lead to 21–17. But the next two times the Steelers got the ball, he had passes intercepted. Miami won and

went on to the Super Bowl. Still, Terry Bradshaw had nothing to be ashamed of. He had shown that he had all the equipment needed to eventually bring Pittsburgh a world championship.

As Dallas Cowboy assistant coach Ermal Allen pointed out, "Bradshaw has the quickest release in pro football— quicker than Joe Namath's. He's also the most aggressive quarterback I've ever seen. He has the guts of a burglar."

The guts of a burglar and a Golden Arm—look out, NFL!

John Brockington

With only minutes remaining in a 1971 game, the Chicago Bears scored to tie the Green Bay Packers 14–14. Green Bay got a tremendous kickoff return, all the way to Chicago's 39-yard line. But the Packers knew they had to advance the ball at least 20 yards if there was to be any certainty that aging place-kicker Lou Michaels would kick a field goal.

Rookie Packer quarterback Scott Hunter knew exactly what he was going to do to pick up the yardage needed to win the ball game. He was going to call on another rookie, fullback John Brockington. After all, the 6-foot-2, 225-pound Brockington had been the most consistent Packer ball-carrier all season,

running with what one opponent called "savage determination."

On first down Hunter handed off to John on a sweep around right end. The Bear defense swiftly swung to that side, so instead of running into all those would-be tacklers Brockington pivoted sharply and turned upfield *inside* his tight end's block. He gained six yards.

On the following play he hit a big hole at right tackle, shot into the secondary and, with the help of a partial block on Bear linebacker Dick Butkus, went for a 13-yard gain to the 20. On the next play John was hit the instant he took the hand-off, a three-yard loss.

On his fourth carry in a row, Brock-

The Packers' John Brockington carries the ball against the Chicago Bears.

ington circled wide to the right, as if he were a decoy. Hunter faked a hand-off to his halfback, then turned and pitched out to Brockington. John turned upfield, lowered his shoulder into the corner-back who crouched to hit him, then drove ahead for six yards before a line-backer and a tackle pulled him down.

With the ball on the 17-yard line and only a litle over a minute left to play, Hunter sent Brockington straight ahead to be sure the ball stayed in the middle of the field. Brockington gained two yards. Then Michaels came in and kicked the three pointer that gave the Packers a 17–14 victory. But it was the Packer offensive linemen and rookie John Brockington, with his five successive carries against the brutal Bear defense, who had done the job at a critical time.

"Brock has intense determination," said Charlie Hall, John's roommate on the Packers that first year. "I think he's going to become the greatest running back ever to play this game. He *lives* to excel."

Brockington's coach at Thomas Jefferson High School in Brooklyn, N.Y., wasn't always sure of that, though. John grew up in Canarsie, a predominantly white, middle-class section of Brooklyn. He followed his older brother Freeman to the football team at Thomas Jefferson, which year after year fielded one of the best high school squads in the east. At first Freeman was more serious about the sport and he became an all-city half-back. John loved the game—but on his own terms. He didn't always think it was necessary for him to show up at practice.

"I'd be coming out of school in the afternoon," confessed John, "and I might feel tired. Some days you just don't feel like practicing, so I'd just take off and go home."

When he began dating a classmate named Jackie, who later became his wife, John's absences from practice increased.

"But one day, after missing practice the day before, I showed up and the coach called me in. He had the two team captains there. 'You're hurting the team,' the coach said. 'You have a bad attitude, and we're going to have to drop you.'

"I was really scared. I didn't want to be thrown off the team. Then the coach said I could have one more chance. I think he was just trying to scare me— and he did. I have never missed a football practice since then."

In John's senior year Jefferson High tied for the city championship as he rushed for over 1,000 yards and made high school All-America. Syracuse University coach Ben Schwartzwalder was interested in him, but John had to improve his grades to qualify for an athletic scholarship. So Syracuse sent him to Manlius Prep, a military school, for a year.

"Man, in some ways that was a real bummer," recalled John. "Formations, reveille, that garbage. But I picked up some good study habits, and we played college freshman teams, so I was lucky."

But when he finished the year at Manlius in June, the Army was showing an interest in Brockington, and Syracuse wouldn't officially accept him until August. John feared he would be drafted before then. However, Ohio State coach Woody Hayes had seen films of the full-

Brockington dresses for a game.

did not have to worry about his new position after the second game. He was hurt and sidelined for the season.

By the time spring practice began, Brockington was well again, and assistant coach Rudy Hubbard asked him what position he wanted to play. John said fullback. "You know what you're up against?" asked Hubbard. "Yeah," said John, "but I can beat out Otis."

John thought he outplayed Otis both in spring practice and again in the fall. But he remained the number two fullback. Frustrated, Brockington went to coach Woody Hayes.

"Woody dropped a bomb on me," said John. "He told me that Otis was the best fullback he'd ever had, bar none, and that he had total confidence in him. He told me Otis was a better back than me."

John decided to transfer to another school. "If I couldn't get over as a football player, there was nothing I could do. You don't talk your way into a position; you play your way into it. I had done that, but I couldn't buck Woody."

Fortunately for John Brockington, for Woody Hayes and for Ohio State, assistant coach Hubbard talked the young fullback out of transferring. Otis graduated, and Brockington became the first-string fullback in 1970. Then he got to carry the football more times in one season (216) and gained more yards (1,041) than any other fullback in Ohio State history. "That last year made it all worthwhile," said John.

Pro scouts called him "the best fullback in the country." Both the Packers and the Bears wanted him. Chicago had an earlier pick than Green Bay, but the Packers wanted Brockington so badly

back from Brooklyn, and one day he just showed up at John's home.

"Can you dig it?" John said. "I mean, there I was, a nobody. And this big-time guy comes to visit me. That man . . . I remember him saying I'd have an offensive line in front of me that I wouldn't even be able to *see* over. I said, 'Yeaaah.' "

Hayes was persuasive and John left Syracuse in the lurch to enter Ohio State.

Although he was built like a fullback, Brockington had been timed at 4.39 seconds in the 40-yard dash—and very few halfbacks can do better than that. As a sophomore he played halfback, because Ohio State already had a good fullback in junior Jim Otis. Brockington was not at all pleased, because in the Ohio State system the fullback does almost all of the ball-carrying. But John that they made a trade to get an earlier pick than the Bears.

Brockington was soon reminding Packer fans of Jim Taylor, the great Packer fullback of the early 1960s who helped lead the Pack to NFL championships. Like Taylor, Brockington would just as soon run over defenders as around them. In 1971, John averaged 5.1 yards per carry, and he carried the ball for 1,105 yards. He was only the third rookie in NFL history to rush for over 1,000 yards, and he was named the NFL's Rookie of the Year.

The 1971 Packers were rebuilding under coach Dan Devine, who was a rookie in the NFL after a long career at the University of Missouri.

The young team made a lot of mistakes, and so did Brockington. But he also shocked some strong NFL defenses. During one three-game stretch at midseason he picked up over 400 yards against three of the toughest defenses in the league. Starting on the soggy field at Milwaukee County Stadium against the Lions, Brockington banged and battered his way to 111 yards in 16 carries. Against the Bears a week later he rushed 30 times for 142 yards. Then, facing the best defensive line in football, Brockington ran 23 times and gained 149 yards against the Vikings.

"Brockington is something else," Minnesota coach Bud Grant said afterward. "The Packer offensive line does a great job for him, but he did an awful lot himself today. He was running with nothing in front of him at times, and he still managed to get outside. He's as fine a runner as I've seen."

"You've got to like the guy," said veteran defensive tackle George Seals, who was then with the Bears. "He breaks tackles and just keeps coming at you, over and over again."

Green Bay's offensive linemen, who had been frustrated for several years, found that blocking for Brockington inspired them. Said center Ken Bowman, "Before Brock, we didn't have a power runner. It doesn't help to gain four yards on first down and five yards on second unless you have a back who can come up on third down and get one yard when you need it. A tough inside man like Brock makes all the difference in the world."

"He's as hard a running back as I've ever seen," said guard Bill Lueck. "An arm tackle just won't slow him down at all. And the speed he has for his size is just amazing. I tell you, you play with a runner like Brockington and see him breaking his back every play—and

Brockington steps high to break a tackle . . .

it's embarrassing if you miss your block."

Bart Starr, the great Packer quarterback of the championship years who became an assistant coach in charge of the offense under Dan Devine, said that in all his years in Green Bay he'd never seen any rookie work harder than John Brockington. "The mark of a great back is how well he performs after he becomes a star," said Bart. "And I think Brock has the attitude and the drive to be the best."

In 1972 John Brockington proved himself to be the best fullback in the NFC, and under the most difficult circumstances. Coach Devine went almost exclusively to a running attack to move the ball because he didn't have that much faith in second-year quarterback Scott Hunter. But he did have faith in Brockington and halfback MacArthur Lane to power the Green Bay offense. And the Packers, who finished last in the NFC Central Division in '71 with a 6–8 record, finished first with a 10–4 mark in '72. In the season's next-to-last game, against the rugged Vikings, the Pack had to win to clinch the title. That day Brockington banged and slashed and drove for 114 yards on the ground as Green Bay won, 23–7.

The Redskins knocked the Packers out of the playoffs two weeks later by clamping down on Brockington and Lane. But John Brockington walked off the field with his head up. He had rushed for 1,027 yards in his second pro season—the first running back ever to gain over 1,000 yards on the ground in each of his first two campaigns. And he went into the locker room thinking about the future, thinking determined, optimistic thoughts.

35

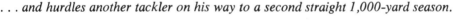

. . . and hurdles another tackler on his way to a second straight 1,000-yard season.

Bob Brown

Robert Stanford Brown stood 6-foot-5 and weighed between 280 and 300 pounds, and he was known as "the Boomer." He had earned a degree in biology at the University of Nebraska and a master's degree in education administration at the University of Pennsylvania. During his first ten years in the NFL, another tough "school," he earned a reputation as the best offensive tackle ever to play the game.

"He is a great—I mean *great*—football player," said Dolphin coach Don Shula, who had coached another legendary offensive tackle, Jim Parker, at Baltimore. According to Shula, Brown was even a better blocker than Parker.

"I'm not a finesse lineman like a lot of tackles in this league," said Brown. "There's nothing fancy about me. I'm about as fancy as a 16-pound sledge hammer. I'm basic.

"From the opening kickoff on, I beat on people. I do it because I want to see some results by the fourth quarter. Those finesse guys are all right, except that in the last quarter their opponent is still trying to get around them. With me, the opponents don't have quite as much left. They're not so sure they *want* to keep coming at me any more. I try to take a toll on them."

On pass blocks, many tackles play the role of a punching bag. They drop back and place their bodies between their quarterback and the onrushing defensive players. These tackles get smacked in the head, butted in the chest or chin, thrown, pushed and yanked at. As long as the defenders don't get to the quarter-back, the tackles have done their job.

Bob Brown's aim was to protect his passer, too, but he went about it differently. He was without question the most aggressive tackle in football. Instead of dropping back on a pass play, Brown often fired into the defensive end, throwing one of his huge forearms ahead of him, digging it into the opponent's stomach or neck or kidney.

"Watch him when he goes to pass block," said Eagle defensive end Richard Harris. "He slams you with both forearms. After a while, that can take the wind out of you."

"The Boomer pulls plen-ty iron," veterans would tell young defensive linemen, warning them that they would have to go *around* Bob Brown, not through him. Of course, the young men didn't always listen. One rookie end who had a big college reputation tried throughout a long afternoon to run over Brown. When it was over, Bob said: "That boy was like a cabbage, all head and no butt, and I ate him."

After playing for the Eagles and the Rams, Brown reported to the Oakland Raider training camp for the first time in 1971. He began warming up by banging his forearms into a wooden goal post. Perhaps he was trying to make an impression on his new teammates, or perhaps he did not care for wooden goal posts. In any case, after several shots from Brown, the post shattered.

Even defensive players on his own team learned to respect Brown. During an early Raider practice, Bob was angered by reserve defensive end Alphonse

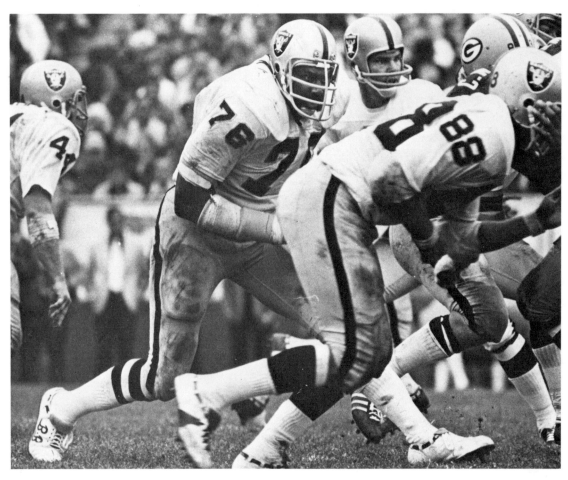

As a play starts, Oakland's Bob Brown (76) sets up to protect quarterback Daryle Lamonica, whose face can be seen just to the right of Brown.

Dotson. Brown told Dotson to stop holding him (although it is legal for a defensive player to use his hands, it is illegal to hold). Dotson did not stop. On the next play Brown clubbed Dotson to the ground with a right forearm to the jaw.

The Boomer did the same thing later to Jet defensive end Gerry Philbin in a preseason game. Philbin had told a reporter that Brown had not played well the last time they had met. Brown read that in the papers. When the two players met·on the first play from scrimmage, Brown dropped Philbin to his knees with

that lethal forearm. The Boomer was even known to fire a clenched fist in retaliation at defenders who played outside the rules.

"It's a simple issue of me–him," Brown said. "Who's the strongest, who's the most determined, who has the highest threshold of pain?"

Brown's threshold of pain was incredibly high. Just 34 days after a knee operation in 1971, Bob was back playing football. As it turned out, he probably resumed playing too soon, because after the season he again needed surgery on that knee.

"I walked out of the hospital," he said after the second operation. "No wheelchair scene. I'll approach the new season with reckless abandon like I always have. There will be no worries, no tape. I won't think about the knee. I might go at a slightly slower pace now so that it won't cost me time during the regular season."

During the 1972 season the Boomer was his old invincible self with the Oakland Raiders. Teammate Gene Upshaw, who was usually playing next to Brown, stood on the sidelines one day and marveled at Brown's play. "He physically dominates a defensive player," said Gene. "Man, I wouldn't want to play against him. Can you imagine the headaches you'd get after he hit you in the head with his arm all afternoon?"

Bob Brown determined very early in life, when he was growing up in Cleveland, Ohio, that he was going to be the best at whatever he tried to do—and that he was going to stay the best.

"When I was a kid we played that old game, King of the Hill," Brown recalled. "You did anything to get on top of the hill. You scratched, kicked, punched, bit, put a thumb in the other guy's eye, I mean anything to get on top. Once I got there, I made up my mind I was going to stay up there—and nobody moved me. It's the same thing with pro football. Right now I'm King of the Hill. And that's the way it's going to be until the day I quit."

Bob grew up in what was known as Cleveland's Black Belt. Some of his childhood friends have gone on to take up residence in penitentiaries. But Bob's neighborhood was better than many. His father owned a delicatessen, and Bob's major childhood problem was eating too much of the calorie-rich delights from the store. Long before he had grown to 6-foot-5, he had grown extremely wide.

"I was the victim of some cruel and humiliating kibitzing by the neighborhood kids," Bob said. "I didn't mind it so much with the boys, but when the girls started heckling me, I had it. When I was sixteen I weighed 290 pounds and, naturally, I had a horrible social life. So I decided to do something about it. I quit eating. For five days I took nothing but vitamins and water, and the weight just rolled off me. I was so hungry I was in pain. But I found out that you can stand pain if you really want something. I wanted to lose weight, and in three months I lost 75 pounds. My social life picked up."

The weight loss did not hurt his play at Cleveland's East Tech High School, where his performance won him a scholarship to the University of Nebraska. There the coaches asked him to put on weight again. Bob simply started eating heavily once more. He also began a workout routine that he followed throughout his pro career—weight lifting and running nearly every day, in season and out. He had no problem at all with football and even got some All-America mentions as a sophomore. As a junior and senior he was almost everyone's All-America guard, possessing amazing speed to go with his strength and determination.

Brown had problems at Nebraska, though. "I found out I wasn't prepared for college at all," he said. "I also found out they didn't care whether I graduated or not. They only wanted me to stay

Brown misses an assignment against the Steelers and all 280 pounds of him come down hard.

eligible for football. An adviser filled in twelve units a semester for me my freshman year. Then I found out I needed 120 units to graduate. No way I could do that in four years, taking twelve units a semester."

From then on, as a biology major and a football player who had to spend a lot of his time practicing, Bob took extra units every semester. And he graduated with a B-plus average in four years, without even attending summer school.

"I was the first one in my family to ever get a college diploma," he said, "and I didn't want to make it as just a C student. Who can brag about a C average?"

The Philadelphia Eagles made this unusual student and unusual football player their top draft choice in 1963. The Denver Broncos of the American Football League also made him their first-round draft pick and offered him $125,000 for three years. A hard bargainer, Bob squeezed a bit more out of the Eagles before signing with them. Brown made the Pro Bowl squad as a rookie tackle and began making All-Pro the next year. But he spent five frustrating years in Philadelphia as the Eagles lost most of their games and changed coaches and ownership. Finally he asked to be traded. He went to the Los Angeles Rams for three

Brown and Les Josephson (34) protect Ram passer Roman Gabriel from Viking Carl Eller.

players who never made good. Brown again made All-Pro that season (1969), and in 1970 he was voted the outstanding offensive lineman in the entire NFC as he helped the Rams reach the playoffs.

Then Bob went to the Ram management and asked for a much better contract. The Rams had just signed quarterback Roman Gabriel for an enormous salary increase, and Bob thought he should be paid at about the same level.

Playing for Philadelphia, Brown keeps a tackler away from the ball-carrier in 1966.

42

The Rams said they couldn't afford to pay an offensive tackle that kind of money. As a quarterback Gabriel drew fans to the park and put points on the board they said.

"Well, then," said Bob, "maybe the Boomer won't block his fool head off, and then we'll see if Gabriel can put those pretty points on the board. The salary you're offering me is certainly not what I'm worth."

He asked to be traded, and the Rams were nice enough to send him to another contending team, the Oakland Raiders. The Raiders welcomed Brown with an open checkbook, and the Boomer responded by playing his usual sensational game of battering, bruising football.

Throughout his career, Bob's stand-up, outspoken attitude tended to earn him a reputation as a troublemaker. Many sportswriters suggested that he was unmanageable, a guy who demanded special treatment.

"I'd be lying if I said it [the criticism] doesn't bother me," said Bob. "I don't lose any sleep because if I lost sleep every time somebody wrote that, I'd never sleep. But it bothers me. There's a tendency to think of athletes as part of a herd, just animals, totally insensitive. But we're people. Big people, but people just the same. When I'm ripped in the newspapers, it hurts me. And I worry sometimes that my folks will see a story and think they didn't raise me right. I happen to think they did a good job.

"All that talk about my demanding special treatment! I've never been pampered in my life. I wouldn't know how to act. I never give less than my best out on that field."

Or anyplace else. Every day when Bob drove his young son, Robert Stanford Brown II, to school, he would tell him: "Don't be ordinary. Anybody can be that. Excel!"

Line coach Dick Stanfel, under whom Brown played with the Eagles, said, "I never coached a man who worked harder than Bob Brown."

"He's just the most devastating football player I've ever seen," said Raider coach John Madden. "He's a super superstar."

Larry Brown

Washington's great running back Larry Brown takes off for the goal with the ball cradled in his arm.

Larry Brown stood just 5-foot-11 and weighed only 195 pounds, but in his first four years in the National Football League he had *averaged* over 1,000 yards rushing per season. Nick Buoniconti, the smallest middle linebacker in the league, appreciated little Larry's running skills after studying films of him as the Dolphins prepared for the Super Bowl game against Washington in January, 1973. Buoniconti shook his head and said, "Larry Brown can run every way he wants to run—power, speed, quick cuts, you name it. This guy is just exceptional. Put him up in the *stands* and he'll still run for yardage."

Brown attributed much of his success to the late Vince Lombardi, who had given him his big chance in pro ball. "I'm a competitor," said Brown. "If I play checkers I hate to be defeated. One thing Vince instilled in me is that anyone can be a loser. But it takes a special person to be a winner."

Yet Larry Brown had wanted to be a winner long before he met Vince Lombardi. He wanted very badly to be somebody, and he seemed very unlikely to succeed.

He was born in Clairton, Pennsylvania, in 1947. His family soon moved to Pittsburgh, where Larry's father was a baggage handler for the Pennsylvania Railroad. Larry and his two older brothers grew up in the ghetto known as "The Hill." "You wouldn't want to stand on a corner there without your friends," Larry recalled. "I went through the same problems of the slums that many young people have had to go through."

But Larry looked for a way out. At first he thought baseball was his answer. Until his junior year at Schenley High School he concentrated on baseball. Then he decided he might do better as a football player. He'd had some success as a "sandlot" running back—in games of tackle football played on concrete. It wouldn't be much of a jump to the grassless, hard-packed high school field if he could avoid the oil that was sprayed on the field to keep the dust down.

As a senior, in his only year of high school football, Larry made honorable mention on the all-city team. But Schenley High School won only two games that year, and Larry was ignored by college football scouts. In addition, Larry had poor grades and no money to enroll in college on his own. Still, he wanted to go to college.

Finally his high school coach arranged a football scholarship for Larry at Dodge City Junior College in Kansas. Dodge City, famous as a lawless place in the Old West, was now a dusty little town far from any large city. It was hardly the most thrilling place for a sharp ghetto youngster to try to be somebody. But Larry made the team and kept his grades up. He set several rushing records for the school in the next two years.

Then his coach, Leroy Montgomery,

got an offer to move to Kansas State University, and he asked Larry to go with him. "I was always impressed with him," Montgomery said. "He was a real hard-nosed kid. I was especially impressed with his blocking. He was a very, very dedicated football player."

Unfortunately for Larry, Kansas State had a running back named Cornelius Davis who had rushed for over 1,000 yards with a winless team the year before. Larry would be a blocking back for Davis in 1967, if he made the team at all.

"They put me with the redshirts [players kept out of varsity competition for a season]," Larry recalled. "I showed everybody what I could do by knocking a few redshirts upside the head. The coaches had to take notice, so they moved me up to the second team. They knew I was trying and that I was a hitter, but they didn't think I could comprehend their system. The opening game was against Colorado State, and I didn't even get in. It was the first time in my life I ever sat on the bench."

He started the following week, though, and went on to rush for 282 yards in nine games. As a senior he did a bit better with another weak club, carrying for 402 yards. These were not the kind of statistics to impress pro scouts. But the Washington Redskins took note of Brown's toughness and his quickness. They picked him in the eighth round—after more than 180 other players had been chosen.

That summer (1969) Brown reported to Vince Lombardi, who had just taken over as coach of the Redskins. And immediately Lombardi began screaming at him. "What's wrong with you,

Larry Brown: a fierce competitor.

Brown?" Vince yelled. "Why can't you get off the ball on the count?"

Lombardi did like the way Larry ran once the play developed. He was shifty and quick and he had good balance. But he was slow to move when the ball was snapped, slow hitting the holes. A running back has to start moving a split second *before* the quarterback yells the snap number. Brown was moving a split second *after* the rest of the Redskin offensive unit.

Larry confessed his problem to Lombardi: he was deaf in his right ear.

When he lined up behind the quarterback on the left side, he simply couldn't hear the barked signal. Lombardi put his arm around the young halfback's shoulders and told him not to worry, that he would take care of the problem. "But in the meantime, Larry, always line up on the right side."

A few days later Lombardi had arranged to get a special $400 helmet for his young halfback. Inside the helmet's right earhole was a transmitter that would send sound to an amplifier mounted over Larry's left, or good ear. From the moment he put on the helmet, Brown became one of the quickest halfbacks in the league at getting off the ball. At times he actually seemed to hit holes before blockers could open them. This brought a smile to Lombardi's face.

But Larry had still not solved all his problems. After a passing drill, Lombardi growled, "He can't play for me—he can't catch the ball!"

Brown had never been a receiver in college, and he had no experience catching passes. He dropped almost everything thrown his way the first week or so with the Redskins.

"But he worked hard to learn," said Bill Austin, an assistant coach under Lombardi. "Larry listened to advice from the coaches and other receivers and began concentrating on 'looking the ball' into his hands. At the end of his rookie season we checked our figures, and Larry had caught 38 of the 42 passes thrown to him."

He had also rushed for 888 yards that first year and was finally being noticed. The next season, 1970, began on a somber note as Brown's mentor, Vince Lombardi, died. Larry still managed to

45

justify Lombardi's faith in him, gaining 1,125 yards.

After the season Larry said, "I owe Vince everything. I wouldn't be playing if it wasn't for him. When I had a fumbling problem, he made me take a football home and carry it around with me. It was very embarrassing to my friends, but not to me. He taught me 'winning is the only thing,' and you can't win fumbling. He taught me to believe in myself, to believe I could make it. He molded me into what I am now."

In the 1973 Super Bowl, Larry doesn't get far against Miami's Manny Fernandez (75).

In 1971, Brown's rushing total fell off to 948 yards. Sonny Jurgensen, the Redskins' great passing quarterback, was injured and lost for the season. His replacement, Billy Kilmer, was a fine leader but not as sharp a passer. So the defenses keyed more on Brown.

In 1972, Jurgensen was again injured early in the season, but this time Kilmer learned how to hit on enough short passes to keep the pressure off Brown. Larry responded by rushing for 1,216 yards in the first 12 games. The Redskins had already clinched a playoff spot, so Larry sat out the last two regular-season games with a nagging injury. He lost the league rushing title to O. J. Simpson, but he was ready for the crucial playoff.

Washington won decisively over Green Bay in the first playoff round and then trounced the world champion Dallas Cowboys to win the NFC title. In both games Larry Brown was the big man on the Redskin offense. Then came the 1973 Super Bowl against the Miami Dolphins. The Dolphins keyed on Brown, stopping him again and again for short gains. Kilmer couldn't complete his passes, and the Dolphins won 14–7. But at least the Redskins got to play in a championship game for the first time since 1945, and Larry Brown was largely responsible for that achievement.

"He does things now that all good runners do," said a Redskin assistant coach. "From the instant he takes the hand-off, Larry uses his quick eyes and quick feet to find the first crack in that wall in front of him. *Swishh,* he's through! And when he turns upfield and has that goal line in sight, he really turns on the speed. He actually seems faster than he is once he spots that goal line."

"And he has incredible determination," guard Vince Promuto once said. "Watch him early in a game. See how he punishes himself to get that extra yard. He never saves anything. Then look at Larry in the fourth quarter. He's still busting tackles!"

One of the finest performances of Larry's career came in a 1972 game against the Giants in which he rushed for 191 yards. Using his tremendous balance, powerful legs and great determination, Brown picked up many of those yards on his own.

"I hit him on the line of scrimmage three or four times," Giant middle linebacker Ron Hornsby said afterward. "And every time he got by me. I don't know how. I never saw a back with such balance. You can't knock him down. We shut down everything else the Redskins had today, but we lost because we couldn't contain Brown."

Larry scored two touchdowns that day, one on a seven-yard pass reception, the other on a 38-yard run where he simply sliced through the Giant defense before the linebackers and secondary could close down on him.

Brown rambles against the New York Giants in 1972 as center Len Hauss (56) looks for a block.

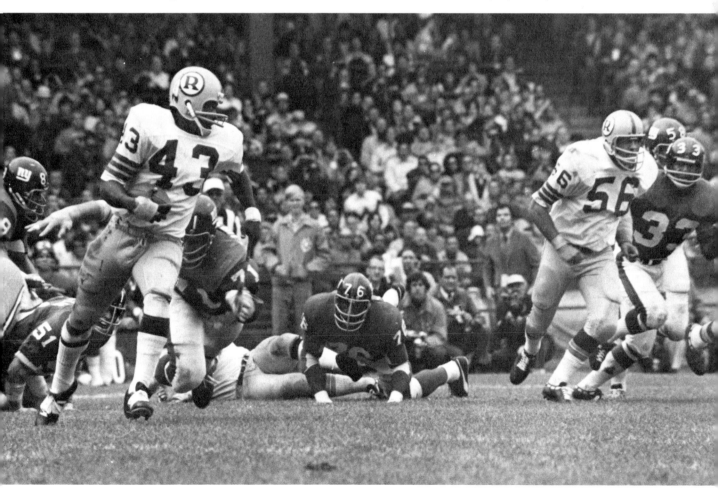

Brown takes a breather during a hard game.

"He's not a power runner," said linebacker Pat Hughes. "He just picks and slides and goes. When you hit him, he relaxes his body and you think he's going down, then—boom!—he's flying again. He never quits."

Some people figured the ferocity of Brown's style would cut short his career, that the pounding he took would take its toll and force him to retire early. It had happened to many great running backs in the NFL—Gale Sayers of the Bears was the most prominent example.

"A running back's only supposed to have three or four years before he starts on the way down," Larry said during 1972. "The key for me is being quick, changing direction on a dime. I'll have to keep my legs healthy, but who's to say I won't still have my legs when I'm 30? I don't take as much punishment as people seem to think."

Punishment or not, Larry Brown still had a few years to become the "somebody" he wanted to be. He had come a long way from his unremarkable high school and college days, but he still wasn't satisfied.

"For a long time people kept thinking of me as only an average back," Larry said. "I want to go beyond that. Everybody's got a big-back theory, but it's not size that makes the back. It's heart and determination. Man, I learned to run when I was a small kid in the ghetto. Nobody gave me anything. Everything I got, I had to work for myself. I'm still working."

Dick Butkus

Coach Vince Lombardi was showing the film of a Chicago Bears game to his championship Green Bay Packers. The Packers were preparing to play Chicago early in the 1965 season, and in the film the Bears' young middle linebacker, Dick Butkus, seemed to be stopping the opposing team all by his large, violent self. Smashing through blockers on running plays and dropping back swiftly to cover passes, he made tackle after tackle from sideline to sideline.

Abruptly Lombardi stopped the film. "Let's smear this kid's face," he growled.

On Sunday the Packers sent swarms of blockers to smear Butkus. He tossed them aside time after time and then *he* smeared the Packer ball-carrier. Walking toward the locker room at the end of the game, Lombardi mumbled to no one in particular, "Butkus is the best who ever played the position."

That was high praise indeed from Vince Lombardi—particularly when you realize that Butkus was only a rookie that season. Dick had made a few mistakes during his first three games. But by the time the Bears met the Packers, he and the rest of the Chicago defense had come together. The Bears lost only two of their last eleven games. Dick led the team both in interceptions and fumble recoveries. Unfortunately, no one recorded the number of fumbles he caused with his vicious tackling.

A 6-foot-3, 245-pounder with amazing range and agility, Butkus played like

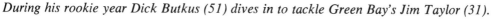

During his rookie year Dick Butkus (51) dives in to tackle Green Bay's Jim Taylor (31).

a man driven by demons. Dick was so ferocious that even in practice he showed little affection for offensive players, and they never looked forward to facing him.

"Scrimmaging against Butkus isn't exactly tranquilizing," said Brian Piccolo, the young Bear halfback who later tragically died of cancer. "When Dick is on the other side of the scrimmage line glaring at you with those boiling eyes, it makes you wish you could change places with the equipment boy."

Butkus liked to hit opponents high, but it tended to hurt them all over. Cardinal halfback Johnny Roland recalled one of the first times he happened to run into Butkus: "I was running up instead of low, as I should have been, and he met me head-on—crash! I have a scar under my lip to this day where he shattered my face mask."

Charlie Sanders, Detroit's great tight end, had some monumental battles with Butkus. In one game Butkus drove his helmet into Sanders' back just as Charlie caught a pass. Sanders rose slowly, trying to regain his breath. But he came right back and caught another pass in Butkus' area. Again Butkus hit him immediately, and somehow Dick's finger found its way through Sanders' facemask and into his eye. According to the Lions, Butkus started three fights that game, and afterward Detroit general manager Russ Thomas complained bitterly about Butkus' violent play.

Sanders simply smiled and said, "Dick's just a maladjusted kid."

Although Dick always insisted that he never went out of his way to try to hurt anyone, he did admit that he liked to remind opponents of his presence.

Early in another game against the Lions, the players on both teams converged down near the 20-yard line under a Detroit punt. But Dick and Lion center Ed Flanagan were still near midfield slugging away at each other. Since he would be facing Flanagan's blocks all afternoon, Dick explained later, "I just wanted him to know he was going to be in a game."

What Butkus' passion was all about, of course, was stopping first downs, and no linebacker did it better. In a 1971 *Sport* Magazine poll of 26 NFL quarterbacks, Butkus was far and away the first choice as best middle linebacker in the league. Many experts agreed with Vince Lombardi in thinking that Dick was the best ever.

"I don't look forward to playing against Butkus," admitted Bengal quarterback Virgil Carter, "because as an ex-Bear I have been around him enough to know how serious his approach to football is. He is so intense that it is a little frightening. And he has a kind of inbred understanding of football that seems to get him to the right place on every play."

"He really makes a study of offenses," said Ram quarterback Roman Gabriel. "He does a lot on his own. The Bears' defense follows his example. He might drop off 20 yards to cover a pass or be three yards off the line of scrimmage to break up a sweep. And he's so strong it's hard to run right at him. You wonder how he can do all this—and how you can get at him. I don't think his skills all come from natural ability. He has to have a fine defensive mind."

When Butkus first joined the Bears, many people wondered if he was smart enough to be a great player. In his sen-

Houston's Donnie Davis runs into Butkus during a 1971 game and loses the ball.

ior year at the University of Illinois, Dick was a two-time All-America and was wanted by every pro team in football. In talking with a writer, he said the only reason he had gone to college was to become a professional football player. This statement caused critics to label him a dummy, and got Dick in trouble at school.

"I got called in by the university president for saying that," an annoyed Butkus said later. "Well, it was the truth. I didn't have any identity crisis as a kid. In the fifth grade I knew what I was going to be—a pro football player. I worked hard at becoming one, just like society says you should. It said you had to be fierce; I was fierce. It said you had to be tough; I was tough."

Butkus had to work hard to complete four years at Illinois. And when you consider his high school preparation for college, Dick's accomplishment was no small thing. He grew up on Chicago's South Side and went to a vocational high school, where many of his subjects entailed working with his hands in shop classes. He also learned to work with his body, though, playing fullback and middle linebacker. A pro scout who saw Butkus in several high school games said, "I wish I could sign him to a contract right now."

Illinois hadn't had an outstanding football team in years when Butkus joined the varsity in 1962. Even in his sophomore season, the Illini won only two games. But the following year he led the team to the Rose Bowl.

A year later the Bears made him their first draft choice. Butkus quickly proved that there should be no question about his intelligence. Soon he was named defensive captain of the Bears and called many of the defensive plays.

"He's uncanny at knowing when to call an audible," Viking assistant coach Jerry Burns commented on Dick's skill at changing the defense at the line of scrimmage just before the snap. The fact is that Dick had studied the game so thoroughly that he seemed to know where a play was going *before* the opposing quarterback did.

"I can see it all about to happen," Dick once said. "At the snap I somehow know, most of the time, just how the flow of the play will develop. It's all there in the backdrop in front of me. I stare right through the center and the quarterback, right through their eyes, looking for keys. They are very tiny

51

As defensive captain of the Bears, Butkus calls for some defensive adjustments before the snap.

keys, believe me. Tiny little twitches of their shoulders and heads and feet and eyes. There's just this split second before it all starts to move when you put these keys together—and you *know* how it's going."

An illustration of Dick's football knowledge and attention to detail oc-curred in one game against the Red-skins. The Bears were trailing 15–9 and were ready to try a field goal. Dick, one of the outside blockers behind the line, ran on the field and reported to an official as required. He also reminded the official that he was an eligible re-ceiver, even though he wasn't wearing a number ordinarily worn by a pass catcher. Although few blockers bother to take this precaution, Dick did it automatically just in case anything should go wrong with the field-goal attempt. And something certainly did go wrong. The center's snap sailed over the head of quarterback Bobby Douglass, who was kneeling to hold for the kick. While Douglass dashed after the bounding ball, Butkus released his block and raced into the end zone. He turned, all alone, and waved his arms frantically. Douglass, under heavy pressure from Redskin tacklers, fired the ball wildly. Butkus dove and caught it for the touchdown that gave the Bears a 16–15 victory.

"Talk about giving 100 percent," said former Bear coach Jim Dooley. "Dick wants to give 110 percent all the time. He's unhappy no matter what kind of game he's had. I don't think he even realizes when he's had a good game, much less a great one. He always thinks he could've played better."

"I simply love football," Dick has

On a broken field-goal play, Butkus dashes into the end zone to catch a pass and win for Chicago.

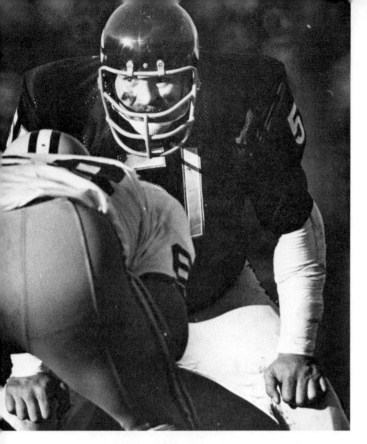

Ever alert, Butkus lines up for another play.

said. "I've tried everything to learn to be more cultural. I've started reading Shakespeare. I've even started reading sportswriters," he chuckled. "But I still love reading offenses most of all.

"I think I've always been nuts about this game. And every time I play a game, I play it as if it was my last one. I could get hurt, even though I never think about that. But if I ever do get hurt, for keeps, I want to go out swinging. I wouldn't want my last game to be a lousy performance."

In the meantime, he took care to see that his family would be in solid financial shape by earning an income outside of football that surpassed his salary with the Bears. He was as dynamic in television commercials as he was on the field, and advertisers loved to use him.

Butkus lived with his wife Helen and their three children in a Chicago suburb of attractive but simple homes. Dick also bought his aging parents a house a few doors away from his own. When he wasn't spending time with his family or doing commercials, Dick devoted much of his offseason time to working out. He had a special workout room built onto his house, which contained $2,400 worth of training equipment. His exercises were designed to keep his heavy muscles toned, to strengthen his knees (both of which had been operated upon) and to keep his weight from going over 245 pounds.

Football was not merely his business, it was his life. And Butkus planned to play football just as long as he stayed healthy. When he began losing his quickness and could no longer effectively cover the middle linebacker's pass responsibilities, he felt he could switch to center on offense. When he got too old or too scarred to play center up to his standards, Dick thought he might turn to coaching.

"When I was younger," he once said, "I wanted a lot of money. But as you get older, you realize there are other things in life. It seems like we judge everyone in this society by how much money they make. Money is fine, but it's not everything."

The thing that was most important to Dick Butkus was, very simply, how well he performed on a football field. "My goal is to be recognized as the best," he said. "No doubt about it. Anybody and everybody makes one All-Pro team or another. You read magazines before the season starts and they're full of All-Pro this and All-Pro that. Everybody's All-Pro. But when they say middle linebacker—I want them to mean *Butkus!*"

Larry Csonka

It was Super Bowl VII in January 1973, and Miami fullback Larry Csonka demonstrated one important reason why the Dolphins had won 16 games in a row and were playing for the world championship. The Dolphins had built a 14–0 lead against the Redskins in the first half. But now, midway through the third quarter, they were having trouble moving the ball. No one was surprised when they called on Csonka. During the regular season he had piled up 1,117 yards rushing on an amazing average of 5.2-yards-per-carry.

Quarterback Bob Griese called a draw play, faking a pass, then handing off to Csonka, who headed up the middle. The blocking was perfect, and Csonka popped through for 12 yards before being brought down on a shoestring

The Dolphins' Larry Csonka is hard to stop—even when grabbed by his shirt-tail.

tackle by the Redskin free safety. On the next play, off left guard, the blocking was not as crisp. Csonka powered into the hole and was hit around the thighs. The 6-foot-2, 237-pound fullback broke that tackle by pumping his massive thighs, then broke a second tackle.

Suddenly Csonka was in the clear. He lengthened his stride and ate up some 40 yards before Redskin cornerback Pat Fischer, who weighed all of 170 pounds, cut in front of him to try and bring him down. Fischer's mistake was coming at Larry high. Csonka threw his right forearm into Fischer's chest, up under his chin, lifting the cornerback off the ground and flinging him aside. Csonka got nine more yards—for a total of 49—before being downed by several pursuing Redskins. Csonka rushed for 112 yards in that game as the Dolphins went on to win the championship, 14–7, a typical performance for him and for them.

"I like a physical game," Larry once said, and he played it physically by running over people more often than he ran around them. In one game, he clobbered a little defensive back with his forearm and became probably the only man ever to be penalized for unnecessary roughness while carrying the ball.

"I'm a third-and-two runner," Csonka explained, "and I like it when it's a physical game right down to the fourth quarter. It's no fun when you're way out in front or way behind. I like it when it's tight. That's when you're earning your money. Football is total expression for guys who don't know how to express themselves any other way.

"But, hey, I *like* people. Some people think I'm a brute, with my knuckles dragging on the ground. I've had people hesitate to come up to me because they weren't sure what I'd do. I hate that. They don't know me."

Csonka was anything but a brute off the field. He expressed himself verbally just as forcefully as he did carrying the ball—and with equal fearlessness. One of his pet peeves was the concrete-hard artificial turf that had been installed in many stadiums. He knew his complaints would not make him a favorite with team owners, who found artificial turf much cheaper to maintain. But Larry spoke out anyway.

"With the development of the Poly Turf we play on in the Orange Bowl," he said, "technology is capable of finishing every player in the league years before his time. Hell, I haven't been hurt when hit—just from being landed on. I feel like my ribs are coming out of my throat on that artificial turf. Let the engineers play on it. Let the owners play on it. I hear there's a guy off somewhere working on a different weather-resistant surface. It's called grass. God bless him."

Another of Larry's complaints was President Nixon's close association with football. "I have no hassle with Mr. Nixon," he said. "Who am I to knock a fan? What I object to is that when it comes from the President, people assume that football is just naturally wonderful for everyone.

"Parents start pushing a kid toward the game without realizing the dangers in it. You see it in these Little Leagues with their poor equipment and poor coaching. Some 25-year-old frustrated jock making kids run 8,000 laps. A kid gets his nose broken and the coach yells at him when he cries, calls him a coward and shames him. Maybe a kid believes he can't compete, that he *is* a coward. If a kid's not ready to hit or be hit, he shouldn't have to."

Lawrence Richard Csonka knew about broken noses. He suffered his first one on his father's 18-acre farm in Stow, Ohio. Larry was bent over making sure that a steer could reach its feed when the animal snapped up its head and cracked him in the nose.

A few years later he broke his nose again during a high school wrestling match. Larry had lifted his 240-pound opponent up over his head to throw him to the mat. "But once I got him up there I couldn't handle him too good," Csonka said later. "He grabbed me around the neck and jerked me forward. I fell with him on top of me—and landed on my nose."

Larry and his younger brother slept in an attic that was so cold in winter that "I could watch my breath go the length of the room," said Larry. "I had a runny nose the first ten years of my life." He also had a lot of chores to do, and when he misbehaved his father made him kneel bare-kneed on corncobs.

"My father was very, very strict," Larry recalled. "He made me hoe beans until I wanted to hit him with the hoe."

But Larry's father was not a man to fool around with. He worked days at the Goodyear plant in Akron, Ohio. Sometimes at night, he earned extra money as a bouncer—keeping order and throwing troublemakers out of the tough local bars. All of the Csonkas—uncles, cousins and so on—were tough. "My father's in his fifties now, and he's still got a 34-inch waist," Larry said proudly.

"And he can still hit you quicker than you can think about it."

Csonka played just about every position on his high school football team, finally settling in as a fullback and linebacker his senior year. He ran like a tank as a fullback and hit like a tank as a linebacker. His coach had once played for coach Ben Schwartzwalder at Syracuse University and helped convince Larry to attend Syracuse as well.

After a fine year as a fullback on the freshman team, Csonka reported to the varsity and Schwartzwalder promptly made him a linebacker. Larry played the position well in the first three games

Csonka watches a play from the sidelines.

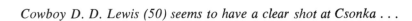

Cowboy D. D. Lewis (50) seems to have a clear shot at Csonka . . .

of his sophomore season, but then the coach decided he needed Larry's strength and drive at fullback.

"Moving Larry was the smartest thing I've done in 23 years of coaching," Schwartzwalder said. "He was a tremendous fullback. His power and determination were incredible."

Indeed they were. He once carried 43 times in a game against Maryland. In another game he gained 14 yards on one play—carrying four tacklers on his back! He worked hard year-round to improve. When he went home in the summer, he constantly worked out with weights. "My mother would raise hell," he remembered. "I used to leave a couple of hundred pounds of weights on my bed, and she couldn't lift them to straighten out the covers."

During his junior year Larry admired

tackle Gary Bugenhagen's forearms, which were the biggest he'd ever seen. Bugenhagen told Csonka he could build up his forearms by banging them into things.

Late that summer Larry's mother called coach Schwartzwalder. "Get him out of here!" she shouted. "Make him come back to school early. He's *too* ready for football. He goes around the house all day slamming his forearms into walls. There's nothing but holes all over the house."

As a senior, Csonka set a Syracuse career rushing record, breaking the records held by Floyd Little, Jimmy Brown, Jim Nance and Ernie Davis. When he passed Little's record with a seven-yard burst off tackle, the referee tossed him the ball.

"I thought the ball was defective or

. . . but a moment later he seems to have disappeared—Csonka has gotten around him.

something and threw it to the bench," said Larry. "I didn't know I'd broken the record. Someone in the huddle told me. I was embarrassed. I guess I should have smiled or something."

Csonka was the Dolphins' top draft choice in 1968 and signed a $100,000 bonus-salary contract. He played in the College All-Star game and was named the Most Valuable Player. During training for the game he met halfback Jim Kiick, another Miami draft pick. They became the best of friends and roommates on the Dolphins. The fact that they communicated so well helped them on the football field.

"Show me the game films of a team and I'll tell you whether the running backs get along," said Csonka. "When Jim and I run a sweep I can sense exactly what he's going to do, how he'll react to the defensive end or the cornerback. We don't have anything in common except friendship, but that makes it work."

In 1968 the Dolphins were still a second-division expansion team. Csonka was held to only 550 yards rushing and he suffered a serious concussion. In the next few games he kept playing although he was having severe headaches. Several games later he was knocked out in a head-on collision with a linebacker. Larry walked off the field, but this time he went straight to the hospital.

His wife Pam stayed in the stands and watched the end of the game. "Larry's convinced me nothing can hurt him," she said later. "He's a very impressive man on and off the field. It wasn't until later that I found out the injury was a lot more serious than I thought."

Playing with a concussion might have caused permanent injury. But Larry was lucky. The headaches gradually went away, and when he got back into the game Larry wore a special shock-resistant helmet for a time.

In 1969, Csonka rushed for 566 yards as the Dolphins continued to struggle. Then in 1970 coach Don Shula came in and revamped the Dolphins. In Shula's first year Larry became the number two rusher in the AFC with 874 yards. The following year he went over the 1,000 mark and, with Jim Kiick, helped carry the once-lowly Dolphins all the way to the Super Bowl.

The turning point for Miami in that 1971 season came late in November. The Dolphins fell behind Pittsburgh, 21–3, then bounced back to score 21 points in a row. "That's the first time we've come from way behind to win a big game," said Shula.

Quarterback Bob Griese and receiver Paul Warfield were the stars of the rally. But Csonka's performance late in the game showed how valuable he was.

With just under two minutes to play, the Dolphins, leading by three, took possession of the ball on their 39-yard line. Csonka carried on four of the next five plays, banging off tackle, bulling up the middle, bashing inside the end. The Dolphins needed a first down. They wanted to run out the clock so that the Steelers would not have a chance to tie or win the game. The Steelers knew Csonka would be carrying, and they had one of the meanest defensive lines in the game, led by tackle Joe Greene. But Larry got the first down, and the final seconds ticked away. Miami 24, Pittsburgh 21.

"It gives a man great satisfaction to do something people are trying to stop him from doing," said Csonka. "I love the game, that's all. I love the whole thing, the total experience. Mind and body. And the result is right there at the end. You don't get ulcers playing football.

"Running backs figure to last four to six years. The lucky ones last eight or ten. I'd like to go fifteen. Maybe I'll do the last couple as a defensive end. I'd like to punish some other people the way they've been punishing me. The only thing that really troubles me is that I won't be able to play forever."

Csonka always laughed and shook off his injuries. In one game, against Buffalo, he broke his nose for the ninth time. When he returned to the huddle and leaned over, blood was pouring from his nose. Huge tight end Marv Fleming almost got sick. Csonka only smiled.

"It's a pitiful sight to see Larry come into the training room the day after a game," said a Dolphin assistant. "Able to walk, but barely. The team doctor comes in and just shakes his head." But the next game Csonka would be playing again.

Facing the huge defensive teams in the NFL should have been enough for Csonka. But a few years ago, on a hunting trip in Canada, he faced a different kind of threat. Larry was sleeping out in a tent when a bear started nibbling at him. He woke up and jabbed the bear in the stomach with his elbow, which sent it running.

Larry modestly dismissed the incident. "It was only a little bear," he said with a laugh.

Mike Curtis

In 1968 they began calling Mike Curtis "Mad Dog" and "The Animal." That was his fourth year with the Baltimore Colts, but his first full season as a regular linebacker. It wasn't hard to see how the 6-foot-2, 232-pound Curtis got his nicknames. Once during a midweek workout, Curtis got so upset that he took a punch at center Bill Curry. Curry was more than Mike's teammate on the Baltimore Colts. He was also Curtis' roommate. But Curry punched back, and in moments the roomies were flying at one another.

Coach Don Shula, who was then the head coach of the Colts, separated the two players and excused the brief fight as healthy enthusiasm. But Shula became a bit more concerned ten days later. This time Curtis really went berserk during a drill. It was "offense day," when the defense was supposed to simulate the defensive patterns of the next opponent so that the offense could get used to them. Since it was only a practice, the defense was supposed to go easy. Then Curtis suddenly raced up from his outside linebacking position

"Mad Dog" Mike Curtis gets quarterback Roman Gabriel before Gabriel can get rid of the ball.

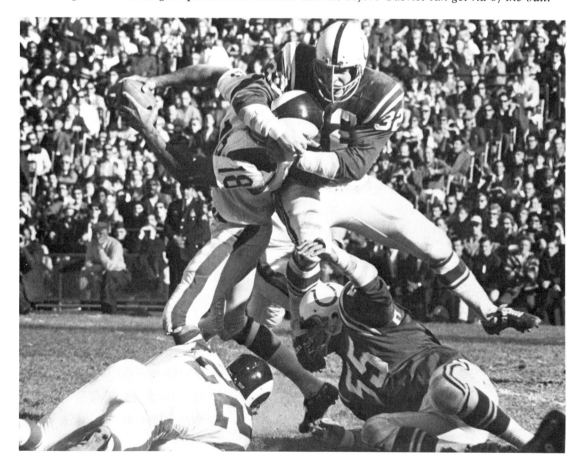

and viciously decked fullback Terry Cole. Shula sent Curtis to the sideline for a full hour to cool off.

"I had blown coverage on Tom Matte and felt humiliated," Mike explained later. "Then Terry came along and really cracked me—knocked my helmet off, in fact. On the next play I really tore into him. I deserved to be sent off. But it's a good thing the coach didn't say much to me then, because I might have slugged *him*. I was fired up and nervous. Something just clicked."

"What Mike Curtis is, more than anything else, is pure football player," said Bill Curry. "Excellence is more important to him than acceptance by teammates or anyone else. He is a man apart, a purist—totally dedicated to football and obsessed by winning."

"I'm never out to hurt anybody," said Mike. "I'm never out to get anybody. I'm just out to play hard and be aggressive and not make a mistake that costs a first down or a touchdown.

"I like to be called aggressive rather than vicious. I'm a competitor, not a bully. I strive to be the best and not break down in my part of the defensive coverage."

Curtis claimed he got his single-mindedness and aggressiveness from his father, who was a supervisor with the public transit system in Washington, D.C. "My father worked hard all his life to support his wife and kids. And when things got a little tough financially, my mother went back to work as a legal secretary. My father says everything was tough when he was growing up. He said when things really got rough, he used to push himself physically just to see how much he could take.

"My parents taught me that hard work and education were the most important things in life. I had a chance to play professional baseball when I got out of high school. But I took a football scholarship instead because a college education went with it."

Curtis' performance as a running back and linebacker at Richard Montgomery High in Rockville, Maryland, earned him more than a hundred college football scholarship offers. He chose Duke University because he thought he might want to be an engineer. He settled instead on history as a major. "I wasn't what you would call a great student," he explained. "I got C-plus grades, but I did graduate."

He was not a great college football player either, but he was a very good one and received honorable mention notice on several All-America teams. He could run 40 yards in 4.7 seconds, fine speed for a man his size. At Duke he played fullback and linebacker, and the Colts drafted him as a linebacker.

But in Mike's rookie season (1965) the Colts traded a fullback and needed a replacement. Mike seemed to be the man for the job. "I was a flop as a running back," Mike said. "I always got into the game late, and I never knew if I was making any progress. That took something off my confidence, which was bad for me, because I have a very bad inferiority complex. I always feel I have to be two or three times better than anybody else just to feel like I'm doing a fair job."

"Mike was miscast as a running

Curtis: a purist totally dedicated to football and obsessed by winning.

back," said a Colt veteran. "He wobbled when he ran the ball, and he had trouble making the cut the way a good pro fullback should. I think he knew it. Maybe that's why he hardly opened his mouth his rookie year. He seldom said much more than hello or goodbye that whole season."

Curtis was switched to outside linebacker the following season and played part time. He loved the contact, and the more he hit, the more sure of himself he seemed to become. He won a starting job in 1967, but then a knee injury in the third game sidelined him for the year.

Mike worked diligently all winter rebuilding the knee, and in 1968 Don Shula called him "the best outside linebacker—maybe the best linebacker, period—in football."

The Colts went all the way to the Super Bowl, thanks partly to Mike's great work on defense. The Jets were so impressed with him in the Super Bowl that they ran most of their plays away from Curtis. But Mike's enthusiasm sometimes got out of hand. He got so excited, especially when the Colts fell behind, that he stopped playing well. On one play he was blitzing—firing into the backfield to tackle quarterback Joe Namath. He saw fullback Matt Snell flare out to his side of the field. Mike should have broken off his blitz and gone with Snell, but he was so intent on hitting Namath that he kept rushing in. Namath calmly looped the pass over Curtis' head to Snell for a nice gain.

"Instead of trying to play football, I was trying to kill those guys," he admitted afterward. "I wanted so badly to beat them that I spent the day trying to hurt them instead of playing my position."

The following season the Colts had their problems on defense, and Shula shifted Curtis to middle linebacker. Many people wondered if he would be able to accept the additional responsibil-

As New York Jet quarterback Joe Namath gets off the ball, Curtis is there.

64

*At the snap of the ball, Curtis is on his way
into the enemy backfield.*

over seven times, the defense was getting more and more tee'd off.

"When we fumbled that sure touchdown out of the end zone, I said 'Good God, what's happening?' When the extra point was blocked, I said, 'How can you win a Super Bowl with a stupid damned trick like that?'"

But this time Curtis wasn't too keyed up to play well. With less than a minute to go and the score tied, 13–13, he dropped back to cover against the pass. The Dallas quarterback threw high to halfback Dan Reeves over the middle. The ball bounced off Reeves' fingertips, and Curtis grabbed the wobbling ball at the Dallas 41-yard line. He shot past Reeves, cut away from another Cowboy tackler and carried 13 yards down to the Dallas 28 before he was brought down. A few plays later, with only nine seconds remaining, Jim O'Brien kicked a 32-yard field goal for a 16–13 Colt victory.

In the bedlam of the Colt locker room afterward, Curtis poured champagne over his head and yelled, "I better enjoy it all now. Next year I could be the goat. But we're champions now. We can say anything."

Then he began talking about Dallas' alternating tight ends in that game, Mike Ditka and Pettis Norman. Both of them, Mike said, had displeased him that afternoon.

"That damned Norman was trying to hold me," said Curtis. "And that damned Ditka kept giving me blind shots. I just wanted one of them to catch a ball high. I was going to tear their guts out [by driving his helmet and shoulder into their outstretched bodies]. I told Norman to cut out that stuff or I was going to break him in half."

ity. They shouldn't have wondered. With his speed and nose for the ball, Mike was perhaps better than ever in the middle of all the action. A year later, 1970, the Colt defense got back together and Curtis got another chance to help win a Super Bowl, this time against Dallas.

It turned out to be one of the sloppiest championship games ever played. Baltimore lost the ball four times on fumbles and three times on interceptions. The Colts even had an extra point blocked. Not surprisingly, Mike Curtis did not remain calm.

"I was yelling at everybody," he said afterward. "I used every four-letter word I could think of and some I invented. When the offense turned the ball

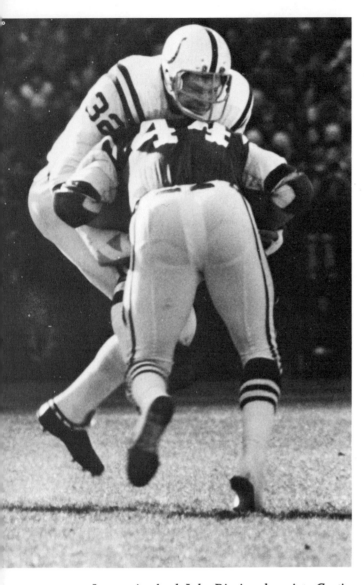

Jet running back John Riggins plows into Curtis.

In 1971 the Colts fought their way to the AFC championship game against Miami. The Colts lost, and Mike almost came to blows with his former coach, Don Shula. Shula was now head coach of the Dolphins. On one play Miami quarterback Bob Griese scrambled out of the pocket and headed down the sideline. Curtis charged over and nearly took Griese's head off with a neck-high tackle. It looked so vicious to one official that Mike was charged with a 15-yard penalty for unnecessary roughness.

Later in the game, Curtis made a tackle that carried him into the Dolphin bench and Shula started yelling at him. "He called me a cheap-shot artist," said Mike. "What was I supposed to do? Walk Griese out of bounds and hold him up? He was still in bounds. When he's running, he's fair game to get his head knocked off. That's what this game's all about."

Obviously, Mike Curtis was not the most popular football player in the league. But that didn't concern him. He was a loner by design. The loss of that 1971 AFC title game and the declining fortunes of the Colts in 1972 didn't make him any more sociable. But he still had his major source of joy—playing the game.

"Football relieves the frustration," he said. "I play it because it's the only place I can commit mayhem without going to jail. I can let loose all my hostilities—and I have a lot—and get paid for it. What could be better?"

For all Curtis' aggressiveness, which some people thought bordered on viciousness, the measure of just how superb a middle linebacker he was came from a Colt player who had starred on Baltimore's great championship teams of 1958 and '59. Looking over the 1970 team that defeated Dallas in the Super Bowl, he said, "You know, there's only one defensive player on this club who could have started for that '59 championship team. Only one—Mike Curtis—because he's so strong and so quick. I've never seen a middle linebacker as quick as Curtis."

Bob Griese

Every young quarterback goes through a difficult period of adjustment in trying to win the respect of his teammates. When Bob Griese came to the Miami Dolphins as a rookie, he was a reserved, introverted young man. Many of the veterans on the team liked excitement—pranks and parties. But Bob refused to participate. The veterans began to call him "Straight Arrow" and cuttingly referred to him as their "milk shake" quarterback. And they snickered when Bob and his roommate, rookie Jack Clancy, decorated their room with potted plants.

None of this bothered Bob. He wasn't

about to change his quiet, conservative personality just because some veteran football players thought he should act just as they did. Griese was determined to win respect in only one way—by his performance on the football field.

He soon won that respect. First he showed that he was an exceptional passer and play caller. And then he showed that he had plenty of courage.

"He isn't afraid to run that ball," said guard Larry Little. "I don't mean scrambling, either. I mean running right up the middle in heavy traffic."

"In one game," added center Bob DeMarco, "we were at the 10-yard line. And down there, where it gets really jammed up, a lot of quarterbacks don't like to run the ball. But Bob called the quarterback draw—which sent him right down the middle—and ran it into the end zone."

"What I'll never forget about Bob was an end-around play," said halfback Jim Kiick. "I handed off to Paul Warfield [who came over from his wide-receiver position to take the ball and sweep around the opposite end]. Bob went around right with Warfield and really stuck it into a big defensive end to spring Paul loose."

Bob was only 6 feet tall and weighed just 190 pounds, but it was soon clear that on the field he would do his part in any situation.

In the end his quiet, "straight" behavior didn't hurt at all. "I think I am more of an introvert than an extrovert," Griese admitted. "I'm not loud or outspoken. And I'd still just as soon be off by myself as be with a group. But if there are a bunch of football players ready to play football, somebody has to

be in command. Taking command of the situation, that's something that somehow I have always been able to do."

When Bob was ten years old his father died suddenly of a heart attack at their home in Evansville, Indiana. Bob's mother sold the family plumbing business and went to work as a secretary to support Bob, his twelve-year-old brother Bill and his eight-year-old sister Joyce. Without a father, Bob listened more attentively to what coaches told him. "I didn't have a father at home to teach me," he said. "A father is really a coach. And coaches became a kind of substitute father for me."

He listened well and played well at quarterback for Rex Mundi High School in Evansville. Soon he was giving advice as well as taking it. One of his coaches called Bob "a kind of player-coach." Griese received football scholarship offers from just about every major college except the one he most wanted to attend: Notre Dame. Bob was a Catholic and Catholic Notre Dame, a major football power, was right in his home state.

Bob finally settled on Purdue (also in Indiana), and in his junior year he gave Notre Dame plenty of reason to regret not offering him a scholarship. The Fighting Irish were the top-ranked team in the nation, but in their game against Purdue, Griese completed 19 of 22 passes to lead Purdue to an upset victory. The following year Griese made All-America and led the Boilermakers into their first Rose Bowl ever, then to a 14–13 victory over Southern Cal.

"Purdue had fine teams for a lot of

As Purdue quarterback, Bob Griese carries the ball against a powerful Michigan State defense.

years without ever going to the Rose Bowl before," Bob said. "I'd say that win and the one over Notre Dame were my biggest thrills in college."

Joe Thomas, then the Dolphins' director of player personnel, went down to see Bob in the locker room after the Rose Bowl. "I had been watching him since he was a sophomore," said Thomas, "but that was the first time I had talked to him. You could see he was going to be a good one—quick feet, quick arm—and he had that fluid way of moving, like a thoroughbred. With a quarterback, though, you want to get an impression of his personality and intelligence.

"Bob was very wide-eyed and alert,

and he had a way of looking straight at you that I liked. After a Bowl game, some of those All-Americas are in a hurry. But Bob wasn't in any hurry to leave. He didn't do a lot of talking. He listened—he revealed an intelligent attentiveness."

The Dolphins had fourth pick in the draft, and Thomas used it to take Griese. June 1967 was a big month for Bob. He got married and he signed with the Dolphins for a reported $200,000 spread over four seasons. The Dolphins had paid more for other rookies, but Bob said, "I wasn't out to bleed anyone. I didn't try to use figures based on what some other guy had gotten."

Bob reported late to his first Dolphin

training camp, and he found himself far behind the Dolphins' three other quarterbacks. In fact, Bob didn't get to play until the final exhibition game. He performed well enough to be moved up to second-string quarterback behind John Stofa. Then, early in the first regular-season game, against Denver, Stofa broke an ankle. Bob stepped right in and completed 12 of 19 passes for 193 yards as the Dolphins won, 35–21.

Even as a rookie, Griese was so knowledgeable about football that he could read defenses. "The Broncos were using a lot of overshifted defenses that were easy to read," Bob said after that first game. "So I called a lot of audibles, and they worked."

Later that season he set a record by throwing 122 passes in succession without an interception. He had an extremely quick release—second only to Joe Namath's, according to experts—that allowed him to wait till the last second before whipping the ball away. And if his protection broke down, as it often did with the Dolphins in those days, Bob's quick feet permitted him to scramble around until a receiver came open. If there was no receiver, he could even run the ball himself.

He was indeed cool and wise for a rookie quarterback, and he finished that first season as the fifth-ranked passer in the American Football League (which merged with the NFL the following year). He completed 50.2 percent of 331 passes for 2,005 yards and 15 touchdowns, although Miami won only four games.

Griese continued to improve during the next two seasons, but the Dolphins did not, winning only seven games in

1968 and '69 combined. Then Don Shula became head coach in 1970. He made some important trades to build a running attack and brought in a great receiver, Paul Warfield, to open up the passing attack. Suddenly Miami had a winner, going all the way to the playoffs. The Dolphins lost to Oakland in the first round, but by only seven points, 21–14.

A year later—in his fifth season as a pro—Griese led the Dolphins to an AFC championship and into the Super Bowl. Although the Dolphins lost the big one

to the Cowboys, they firmly believed in themselves and their future under the talented leadership of Don Shula and Bob Griese.

Explaining his team's tremendous improvement, Bob said, "Marv Fleming is the best blocking tight end in the business. When Shula acquired Marv, he opened up our running game. Our whole offensive line matured with experience, and so did our two big running backs, Jim Kiick and Larry Csonka. Then Warfield, by drawing double-coverage on passing down, made our short and medium passing game more effective.

"Before, we were primarily a passing team. We threw 30 or 40 passes a game because we were behind so much. Now we are a ball-control team—we'll run 60 percent of the time. We throw to make our running game that much more effective. Now those defensive lines can't fly in on us. They have to hold and look for the run before committing themselves."

Griese fires the ball to a Dolphin receiver over the heads of the Dallas Cowboys.

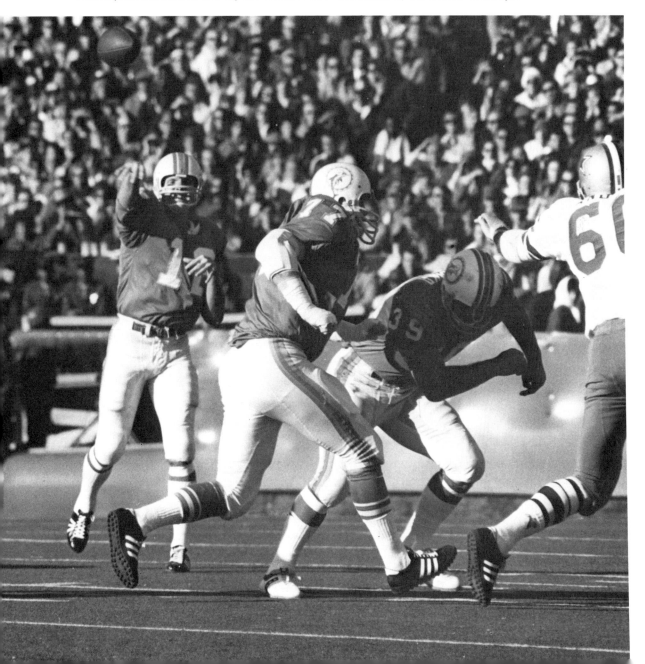

Griese was ideally suited to Shula's ball-control offense, which was similar in style to the one Vince Lombardi coached so successfully at Green Bay in the early 1960s. In fact, Griese's football philosophy was much like that of the man who led those Packer teams, quarterback Bart Starr. Joe Thomas once said, "Listen to the two of them talk and you'd think they were identical twins."

Griese was sometimes criticized, as was Starr before him, for not throwing more bombs. "You don't make a living on the long pass," was Bob's reply. "It is very difficult to throw the long pass. You need a lot of time. The receiver is running dead-away from you, so the throw has to be right on the money. Sure, there's a place for the long throw in a ball game. But you have to be sound on your short and medium passes first."

And you have to be sound on your running game. Griese worked hard to know which running plays to call, when and where. "Before a game," Shula said, "Bob will study the defenses against the run as hard as he will study the defenses against the pass. That's highly unusual for a quarterback."

"Any quarterback would rather throw the ball than hand off," Bob explained. "Anybody can hand off. But not anybody can look at a defense and decide which running plays will work and which won't."

"I'll tell you," former Dolphin quarterback George Mira said, "it is much harder to read a defense against the run than it is against the pass. In a pass defense, there are a lot of people moving around, so you have more keys. In a defense against the run, the defense is set—you don't see as many keys."

The Dolphins were beaten badly by Dallas in Super Bowl VI. But the next season, 1972, the Dolphins made their final step toward maturity. Griese led them to victories in their first five games and relied on the run more than ever as halfback Mercury Morris suddenly emerged as a star. Morris gave the team an outside running threat that made Larry Csonka and Jim Kiick even more effective.

Then Griese broke his ankle in the fifth game. Fortunately, Shula had picked up veteran Earl Morrall and the team was so solid that Miami kept winning, taking all 14 games. The Dolphins, still led by Morrall, beat the Browns in their first playoff game.

But in the AFC title game against Pittsburgh, they ran into trouble. With the Dolphins trailing 10–7 in the third period, coach Shula asked Griese, "Are you ready?"

Bob had been working out for a couple of weeks, but his ankle was still tender. Yet he replied, "I'm ready."

He promptly engineered two touchdown drives, and the Dolphins won their 16th game in a row, 21–17. Late in the game the Dolphins had to run out the clock to preserve the win. When the team huddled for the last series, everyone was talking, excitedly offering suggestions. Griese took command. He instantly silenced the chatter and settled down his teammates. "Shut up," he said sharply. "Let's get this drive going." And they did.

"That's the mark of a leader," said Mercury Morris. "That was his way of telling us to be cool."

Two weeks later Griese started the

Super Bowl against the Redskins. The game was a bruising defensive battle, yet Bob completed his first six passes in succession. Although the final score was Dolphins 14, Redskins 7, the Dolphins led all the way, winning convincingly.

Bob and the team had finally reached the top, winning 17 games in a row. Many players contributed to Miami's record-shattering performance. But in the championship games it was Griese, the "Straight Arrow," who took charge.

Protected by running back Larry Csonka (39), Griese throws a pass in the 1973 Super Bowl.

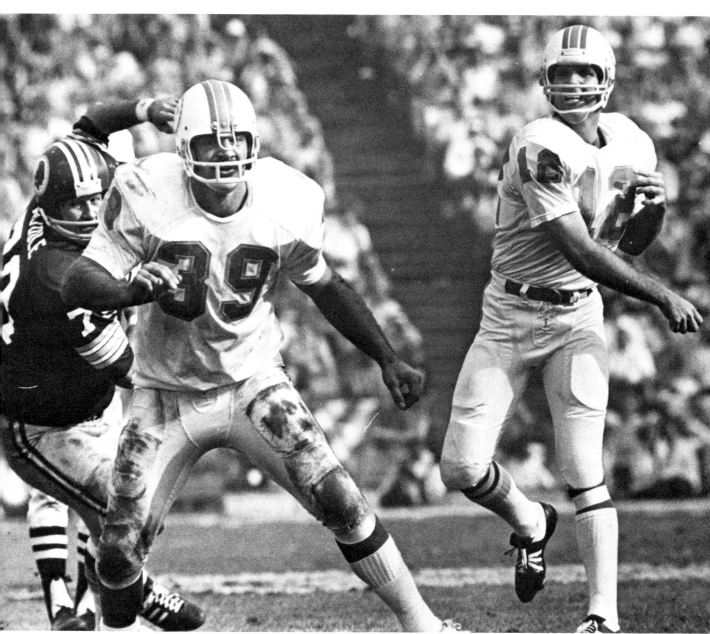

Ron Johnson

As a youngster growing up in Detroit, Ron Johnson's first love was baseball. When he was ten or eleven years old, Ron and his brother Alex, who was five years older, would chalk a strike-zone rectangle on a wall. First Ron would stand beside the rectangle with a bat, while Alex tried to pitch tennis balls past him. It wouldn't take long for Ron to strike out. Then Alex would come to bat. Hitting against his younger brother, Alex did not strike out often.

"I'd throw for maybe two hours," recalled Ron. "My arm would be hurting so that I'd start to cry. Alex would tell me: 'Only a couple more pitches.'"

Alex went on to the major leagues and became the American League batting champion in 1970. Ron never tried out for major league baseball, but the long hours spent pitching to Alex taught him a few things. He learned not to give in to adversity and to punish himself, if need be, to meet a challenge. The same year that Alex won the batting crown, Ron became the first New York Giant ever to gain 1,000 yards rushing in a season.

Two years later Ron rushed for 1,182 yards, scoring nine touchdowns, and caught 45 passes for 451 yards and five touchdowns. He was one of the three or four best running backs in football.

Becoming the best was something of a surprise for Ron. "Going back all the way to grade school, when we were playing football in the streets of Detroit," recalled Ron, "I was never the best in anything. There was always someone bigger, stronger and faster than I was.

My brothers were excellent sandlot and high school athletes. I got a lot of recognition just because I was their younger brother. And I always found myself hustling more than anyone else because I wanted to be considered as good as my brothers."

Johnson began playing organized football when he was 14, joining the West Side Cubs. The Cubs went undefeated until the championship game, but Ron was no sensation, playing part-time fullback. As a sophomore at Northwestern High School, he didn't start a single game.

"As a junior the only reason I started," said Ron, "was because the regular fullback got married and dropped out of school."

Johnson played only four games, though, before being sidelined by an injury. But he kept plugging away all summer with the help of coaches Don Fears and Van Jenkins, who admired his determination. It was well worth the effort for all of them.

As a senior in 1964, Johnson rushed for 980 yards in 89 carries—an average of 11 yards per carry—and scored 14 touchdowns. He was named to the high school All-America team and received about 65 college scholarship offers. He was very proud, not only for himself, but for his father.

"My father only had a fourth-grade education," explained Ron. "He had to stop school to go to work to help his family. When he got married, he dedicated himself to his wife and children, working from dawn till dusk to make us

The New York Giants' Ron Johnson gets away from two opposing tacklers for a big gain.

comfortable. At first he operated a little one-truck hauling business, and then he bought a gas station. He just worked incredibly hard, and he wouldn't even let us help. He wanted his kids to be free. I would go down to the station wanting to work, and he'd say everything was okay, that I should go do something else.

"He loved to watch us play sports, and any time we did well he'd really congratulate us. He lived through us, watching us do things he'd never had a chance to do. That's why I always gave my very best. If I ever wanted to quit, it would've been like quitting on him. After all he'd done for me, I couldn't do that. I couldn't let him down. It gave me an extra incentive."

That incentive carried into the classroom, too. Ron was an A-minus student through high school, and he went to college not merely to play football but to further his education. He never had any idea that he would ever play pro football. He accepted a scholarship to the University of Michigan, one of the strong academic schools in the Big Ten.

On the football field, Ron went through the same experience he'd had in high school. Again he was no "automatic" star. In his first year he was merely the second-string halfback on the freshman team. He got a chance to start with the frosh only because of another halfback's romances.

"A good friend and fraternity brother was starting ahead of me," said Ron. "His girlfriend was back home in Toledo, Ohio. During preseason practice he would skip every Friday so he could go home for the weekend. The excuse he gave week after week was that his grandmother had died. The freshman coach finally started to wonder how many grandmothers a person could have. So the coach demoted him, and that's how I moved up to first team."

Ron had no such luck the next year when he joined the varsity. He was a seldom-used second-team halfback throughout his sophomore season. Johnson was so lightly regarded as a runner that in his junior year the coaches at Michigan decided to shift him to defensive back. But before he could be moved, another running back hurt his knee, so Ron remained on offense. Finally, in his junior and senior years, he became one of the finest ball-carriers in the country. In a game against Wisconsin, he set a Big Ten record by rushing for 347 yards, and his career total of 2,440 yards broke the Michigan record set over 20 years before by the legendary Tommy Harmon.

Pro scouts liked the 6-foot-1, 205-pounder's attitude and style. Johnson had excellent speed to the outside and was a strong, slashing runner to the inside. What's more, he could catch passes. And he obviously took a great deal of pleasure in blocking, something many running backs don't enjoy.

The Cleveland Browns made Johnson their first draft choice for the 1969 season. Their contract offer was too low, though, and Ron became a stubborn holdout until August. Finally the Browns came up a bit and Ron came down a bit, signing a two-year contract that was worth a reported $100,000.

Although Ron came late to training camp, he started in the Browns' first regular-season game in place of Leroy

Johnson watches a play from the bench.

Kelly, Cleveland's All-Pro halfback, who'd been injured during the preseason. In 17 carries against the Eagles, Johnson gained 118 yards, a very promising debut. By the end of the third game he had rushed for 250 yards.

When Kelly returned, Ron began to run less and block more. Then his loss of training time began to show. He had not mastered Cleveland's "option blocking" techniques. Option blocking takes a good deal of practice and experience, for the blocker has to read the defense instantly and decide which of the defenders to block. The ball-carrier who is following the blockers relies on their making the right decision. Ron began making mistakes and began pressing. The more he pressed, the worse he played.

"The coaches feel I've been thinking and hesitating too much," Ron said midway through that rookie season. "I agree with them. I've been too con-

Playing for the Cleveland Browns, Johnson faces a Green Bay tackler in a 1969 game.

cerned about my mistakes. As a result I haven't been slashing in there as I did early in the season."

After twelve games he had rushed for almost 500 yards—not a bad record. But his overall performance was unsatisfactory, and he was benched. Bo Scott started the last two games at fullback. Johnson said afterward, "I couldn't blame the coaches. I knew I wasn't doing the job. I wasn't running the way I can."

Ron was determined to stop hesitating and start slashing again the following season. He had learned to read the option blocks, and there would be no reason for him to hesitate any more. Most experts agreed that Ron had a very bright future.

Then the Browns made a startling move. They traded Ron Johnson to the Giants. In fact, Johnson was actually a *throw-in* in the trade. The Browns got receiver Homer Jones from the Giants. New York got Cleveland defensive tackle Jim Kanicki, and asked if they might also have a Cleveland running back, say Ron Johnson. The Browns agreed.

And suddenly the Giants—who hadn't risen above the .500 mark in six years—were winners. After losing their first three games, they won nine of their last eleven and just missed making the 1970 playoffs. Johnson rushed for 1,027 yards and caught almost 50 passes.

"Last year the only real running game we had was up the gut," said Giant guard Doug Van Horn. "Other teams knew it and played us inside all the time. But now we have Johnson who can go outside. We're running plays we haven't

used in years. Now teams have to respect our outside game, and that makes it a heck of a lot easier for us to run off tackle."

"The performance of Ron Johnson has got to be one of our greatest pluses," said coach Alex Webster. "We knew he was a good football player when we got him, but he's played even better than we expected. And he's so well liked by all the other players that he's been a real leader, right from the beginning. When the team came to camp this summer two weeks late after the player strike, Ron came in and told everyone, 'Okay, now let's play football.' Now, he was new and we had lots and lots of new people, but he came in talking like a coach and everyone responded. For someone that talented, well, he's quite a guy."

"Usually these gifted running backs want all the glory," added Giant safety-man Spider Lockhart. "But Ron doesn't care if he makes the play or not—just as long as *someone* makes it."

After that first season with New York, Johnson and the Giants disagreed about his new contract. But when the 1971 training camp opened and Johnson wasn't there, the Giants were eager to settle. They gave Ron the highest salary they had ever paid a running back. Unfortunately, though, Ron never had a chance to do much in '71. Thigh and knee injuries, which eventually required surgery, limited him to appearances in just two ball games. He gained a mere 156 yards for the season. The Giants collapsed and won only four games.

But in 1972, Johnson was running even better than he had in '70. He showed his old slashing style and even

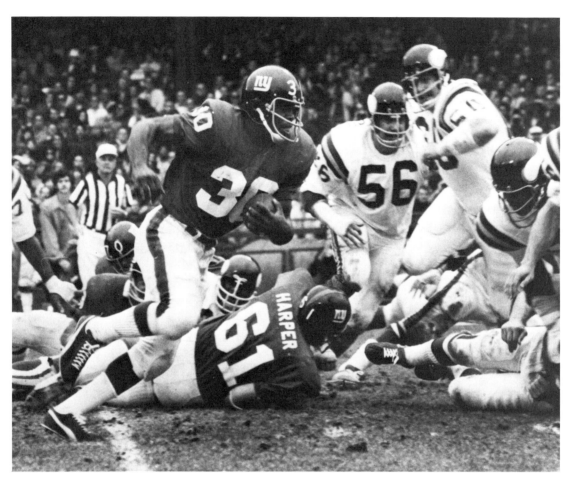

Johnson looks for running room as the Viking defense closes in.

a bit more finesse. He also showed he could be a workhorse when the Giants wanted to control the ball on the ground through the last quarter of a game. He did that magnificently against the Eagles, carrying 36 times—twelve times in the final quarter to preserve a victory. Ron rushed for 124 yards that day, caught five passes for 60 yards and scored all four Giant touchdowns in the 27–12 triumph.

The final drive that consumed much of the fourth period, covered 78 yards and took twelve plays. Johnson carried the ball on eight of them. On the last one he circled out of the backfield, ran past a linebacker trying to cover him, faked out a safetyman in the end zone, then cut left and caught quarterback Norm Snead's 15-yard scoring pass.

"I'm a little banged up," Ron said afterward. "They play a very physical game. But I liked the challenge of handling the ball so much. Every good athlete likes to be challenged. If you haven't got a challenge, there's nothing to live for. For me to be satisfied, I have to give my best. And to give my best, I have to be challenged. That's what makes it all worthwhile."

Greg Landry

Guts—that was the word they used when they talked about quarterback Greg Landry. For example, there was the game against the Eagles in late 1971. The Lions had to win it to stay in play-off contention. Late in the fourth quarter Detroit was losing. Landry drove the club down inside the Eagle 10-yard line. He tried three plays and advanced the ball only to the five.

Now on fourth and goal he calls a pass play. He takes the snap and drops back looking for his receiver, tight end Charley Sanders. But Sanders is covered by two defenders. Landry looks for his wide receivers, but they are covered too.

Greg tucks the ball into his middle and charges forward himself. A linebacker comes up to meet him. Greg lowers his helmet, butts the linebacker with all the power in his 6-foot-4, 215-pound body—and knocks him aside.

Detroit's fearless quarterback, Greg Landry, runs the ball and is downed by Giant John Mendenhall.

Still running low, Greg plows a shoulder into a small Eagle safetyman at the two and bowls him over backwards. At the goal line Greg is creamed by two defensive backs. One hits him low, and the other pops his shoulder pads into Landry's jaw. Landry's momentum carries him into the end zone, putting Detroit ahead, but he falls face down in the mud and lies there unconscious. Two minutes later the Eagles score again to win the game. But Landry, still groggy from his heroic run, hardly knows what's going on.

Lion players had come to expect that kind of gutty play from Landry. Two years earlier, in 1969, he started a game against Minnesota when first-string quarterback Bill Munson was injured. The Vikings massacred the Lions, and Landry took a very bad physical beating. In the third quarter, sprinting out for his life, Greg was smashed in the ankle and got up limping. One of the Lions told him to go to the sideline.

"They'll have to carry me out," answered Greg. "I don't leave ball games."

Landry finished the game, but by then his ankle was so swollen that he couldn't walk on it. He left the stadium on crutches. On Monday the ankle was put in a cast. The cast came off on Thursday, and Greg tried to practice. The swelling had gone down enough for him to squeeze his foot into a high-topped football shoe, but he could hardly limp around. At practice on Saturday, Greg was still limping badly. Coach Joe Schmidt planned to start his third-string quarterback against the 49ers on Sunday.

But during pregame warmups, Schmidt watched Landry and said,

"Look at him. I don't know how he gets back to set up on that ankle. He's actually turning on it!"

Landry started and played the entire game. The 49ers put tremendous pressure on him and for once, he couldn't run away. For every yard he gained passing, he lost a yard being dropped by the big San Francisco defenders. But he kept the Lion offense going and completed one long touchdown pass to Charley Sanders. He connected in several other critical situations to keep drives going, and the Lions won 26–14.

"Landry is a helluva leader," Schmidt said after the game. "He's an example to the other guys. I realize what kind of guts Landry has. His right ankle was swollen so badly that he shouldn't have played at all, let alone try to run on it. But he managed. He was in a great deal of pain and he sacrificed for the team."

Landry's courage didn't earn everyone's admiration, however. During his first three seasons with the Lions, many people said, "He's got more guts than brains." His eagerness to run with the ball did seem foolhardy sometimes. But what Greg lacked was *experience*, not intelligence. It was a problem all good-running college quarterbacks faced when they joined the pros. They had to learn to stand in that pocket and check all their receivers before scurrying off on their own. Landry had always run so well that he never learned to be a classic pocket passer.

Although experience would teach Greg not to be so quick to run, the Lions did recognize his talent and courage. They devised some optional running plays that would allow him to run once in a while with some protection.

Landry wings the ball over the outstretched arms of Green Bay defender Clarence Williams.

Worrying about his running ability, enemy defenses would not be able to rush him as confidently. Soon other teams were encouraging their quarterbacks to imitate Landry. For the first time in years, pro passers were learning to do more than call plays and throw the ball.

"You are going to see a lot of big, running quarterbacks in the next few years," predicted Joe Schmidt. "The Wishbone offense the colleges use is developing them, so there will be a supply. And a running quarterback really puts a load on the defense."

Landry began running a triple-option offense in high school at Nashua, New Hampshire. On the standard play Greg would fake to his fullback, then roll out behind the fullback, with the halfback trailing him. He had the option of passing, pitching the ball to the halfback or running it himself. "Mostly I kept the ball and ran," recalled Greg. "I loved running."

Landry had 4.7 speed in the 40-yard dash, a good arm and good grades. He received many scholarship offers to big colleges like Michigan State, Penn State and Notre Dame. But he chose to go to the University of Massachusetts, where the quality of football played was "a step below the Ivy League," according to Greg.

Why did he go there? "Pro football was beyond my wildest dreams," he explained. "I wanted to be a coach. I figured I should go to a New England school where I could make a name for myself in the area. It would be easier to get a coaching job."

During Landry's three varsity years at U-Mass, as the school is known, the team lost only one conference game. And although the school had developed few pro players, Detroit scouts had their eye on Landry. The Lions passed up such top quarterbacks as UCLA's Gary Beban to draft Landry in the very first round. At the same time, the Lions got reserve quarterback Bill Munson from the Rams in a trade. Coach Schmidt planned to start Munson and bring Landry along slowly. "No way I'm going to start a rookie," he said.

Landry had been surprised that he was drafted in the first round. He gained some confidence by playing in the postseason North-South game where he threw two touchdown passes for the victorious North. "That really began to make me believe I was as good as the quarterbacks from the big schools," he said.

Before the first game of the 1968 season, Bill Munson was injured. Suddenly Landry was the Lions' starting quarterback against the Cowboys in his first NFL game. He proceeded to complete six straight passes against the tough Dallas defense. The last completion went for a touchdown. The pros aren't so tough, he thought.

"I didn't know a thing about defenses," he said later. "I just stepped back into the pocket and threw to the right color jersey on the first series."

At game's end Greg had a bit more perspective on the pros. He had thrown four interceptions and the Cowboys had won, 59–13. He didn't start another game until late in the season, against the Eagles, who hadn't won a single game. Even a rookie couldn't do too badly against them, the coaches felt. The Lions lost, 12–0. "Another humbling experience," said Landry.

The following season, the Lions got their first good look at Landry's courage. Detroit won five of seven games with Greg at quarterback after Munson got hurt. But Landry ran far better than he threw, and it was really the Lion defense that won those games. Schmidt kept telling Greg not to run so much, to stay in the pocket and learn to read defenses. Greg kept promising to try, but he had trouble resisting his impulse to carry the ball himself.

Munson was again the Lions' top quarterback at the start of the 1970 season. In the first game he ran up a 33–0 lead against Green Bay. Then Landry came in to finish up. With the ball on his own 13-yard line, Greg called

83

a sweep to the right. But when the team lined up, he saw the middle linebacker slide over to the side of the sweep. So he took the snap and popped right through the middle himself, going 76 yards on the quarterback sneak.

At midseason the Lions, with quarterback Munson, had a 5–2 record. But Munson was having his problems. Then in the eighth game of the season, against the lowly New Orleans Saints, he threw three interceptions and had trouble moving the ball. Late in the fourth quarter, with the Lions trailing, Landry came in and marched the team 80 yards to set up a field goal that gave the Lions a one-point lead. Although the Saints came back to win on Tom Dempsey's spectacular 63-yard field goal, Landry had earned the Lions' starting quarterback position.

Then Landry took charge and led the Lions to victories in five of their last six games. This earned them a playoff spot. But in the first round against the Cowboys, Greg seemed to freeze up. His fumble led to a Dallas field goal, and he was tackled in the end zone for a safety. The Lions were shut out, and Dallas won 5–0.

Nevertheless, Greg's individual statistics for 1970 were impressive. He completed 60 percent of his passes, gave up only five interceptions and ran for 350 yards. Schmidt stopped telling Landry not to run and put in the options that would allow him to do so with some protection.

Threatened by Packers Leon Crenshaw (70) and Ray Nitschke (66), Landry runs again.

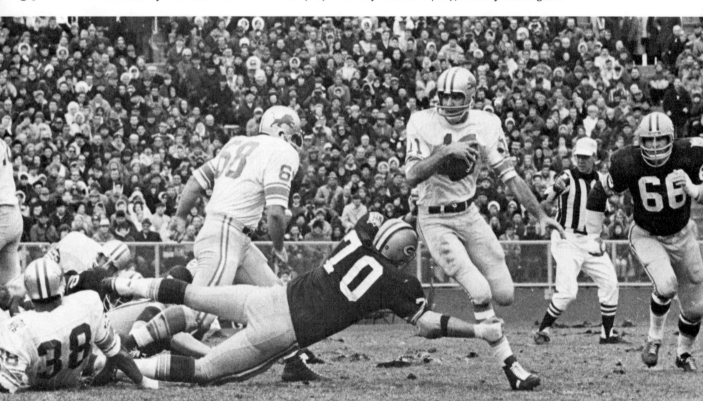

Running with the ball took even more guts than usual for Landry in 1971 because he was playing out his option. After a disagreement with the Lions over his 1971 contract, Landry played the season without signing, hoping to have a big season so that he could negotiate a really big contract for future years. But, of course, if he were injured he might end up making less money. Landry had a big year personally, passing well and setting an NFL record for yards gained rushing by a quarterback, 530 (Bobby Douglass of the Bears broke it by some 300 yards a year later).

But the Lion defense went sour in '71, and the team finished with a 7–6–1 record. The death of Chuck Hughes, who was stricken by a heart attack during a game, shook up the team at midseason, and the Lions won only three of eight games after Hughes died.

Still, Landry had proven his ability in 1971, and the Lions finally gave him his raise. He signed a three-year contract worth about $400,000—a lot of money for a young man from little old U-Mass.

The Lions continued to have their problems in 1972, particularly on defense, finishing second in the NFC Central Division with an 8–5–1 record. But the young Lion offense, while still inconsistent, was indeed high-powered when Greg Landry was right.

"I'm a much better passer than I was two years ago," Landry said in '72, when he passed for 2,066 yards and 18 touchdowns and also ran for 524 yards and nine touchdowns. "Two years ago

Landry asks why the call went against him.

I'd look for my primary receiver, and if he was covered I'd run for my life. Now I look at all my receivers, and even turn to my running backs to throw to. But I'd still rather run than get hit for a loss. You frustrate a defense when they have everyone covered and you run for a first down."

The more Landry frustrated defenses, the harder they tried to nail him when he ran with the ball. But that didn't trouble Landry for one very good reason. It's called: guts.

Bob Lilly

One day when the Dallas Cowboys were getting ready for the 1972 Super Bowl, a writer was standing at practice with coach Tom Landry. The reporter watched Bob Lilly, the Cowboys' 6-foot-5, 260-pound defensive tackle, shoot through the offensive line time and time again.

The writer shook his head in amazement. "After eleven years in the league, he seems better than ever," he said to Landry.

Landry, who once characterized Lilly as "something a little bit more than great," just smiled. Then he said, "If that's possible, it's because his intensity may be even greater now. He's meaner."

Lilly himself wondered if "mean" was the right word. "I don't feel mean," he said. "It's hard to hate a guy that you meet on a Sunday afternoon and won't see again for a year. I never try to kill anybody, that's for sure. I see chances where I can tear up a knee or plaster a face, but I don't take advantage of them. These guys are just shadows out there to me—they aren't people that I have a personal animosity for or anything like that."

Whatever the word, Lilly got the job done. Time after time he broke into enemy backfields to chase the quarterback or cut down a ball-carrier. One of the reasons he seemed unstoppable was his tremendous strength.

"I never realized just how strong Bob was until I was grading films one day," said Cowboy assistant coach Ernie Stautner. "I watched a guard set up to

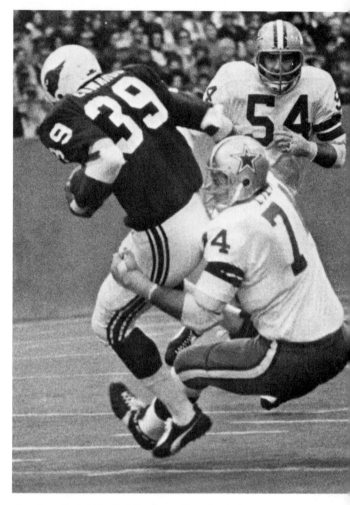

Cowboy Bob Lilly brings down Cardinal Cid Edwards (39) in a 1971 game.

take him. Then Bob made his move. He grabbed the guard by the shoulder pads and threw him bodily off to the side. Bodily! This is really something, because an offensive lineman sets up awfully strong."

Lilly grew up resembling a weight lifter, with massive shoulders and bulging arms and rather spindly legs. He started out on his father's farm near Throckmorton, Texas, lifting bales of hay and calves that refused to walk into the barn. By his junior year in high school he was an outstanding tackle. But he was first spotted by a college football scout playing volleyball. "I'd never seen a big boy who was that quick," said the scout for Texas Christian University (TCU). He made a note to see Lilly the following year when he was a senior.

But the next year Lilly was in Pendleton, Oregon, where his father had set up a land-clearing business. Bob became a high school All-America tackle at Pendleton High. The TCU scout wasn't about to give up, however. He heard about Lilly's performance in Oregon and sent him a postcard offering him a scholarship. Even if Bob didn't make it in football, he would be a great prospect. In high school he had also averaged 27 points a game in basketball and won the javelin throw in the state meet.

"All TCU offered me was my scholarship, plus ten dollars a month laundry money," Lilly recalled. "I had some pretty fancy offers from schools in the Northwest. Some of them offered me a new car and $150 or $200 a month spending money. They even promised to get my father a good job. But I didn't want any of that. I wanted to get back to Texas."

Lilly weighed only 210 pounds when he reported to coach Abe Martin at TCU in September 1957. But with his heavy frame, he would have no trouble putting on weight.

"He was the tallest ol' drink of water I ever saw," Martin recalled. "But he was anxious to get to TCU. He told me that he and a buddy had driven straight through from Oregon in a 1947 Studebaker, never stopping to sleep. I asked him how they ate, and he said, 'Momma made us 60 ham sandwiches and a few gallons of lemonade to carry in the car. We didn't get hungry.' "

Shortly after his arrival, Lilly pulled his car up to the parking space assigned to him and found a Volkswagen sitting there. So he got out of his car, picked up the Bug and deposited it on the sidewalk. When word of his feat got around, he modestly explained, "At no time was the car completely off the ground. First I picked up the front and put it on the sidewalk, then I moved the back end."

Bob performed this trick on small foreign cars perhaps a dozen times at TCU, and it became known as The Lilly Test. Many others took the test, but very few ever passed it.

Lilly himself had his troubles with classroom tests early on at TCU. The main trouble was that he had one course, Water Skiing, which he enjoyed so much that he spent most of his time in it. "A student who can consistently remember his name and the score of last week's game shouldn't have any trouble with grades at TCU," wrote Gary Cartwright, who went there. But Lilly was in danger of flunking out of TCU the second semester of his freshman year until the coaching staff straightened him out.

Playing football was no trouble at all. Bob quickly grew to 250 pounds and played better than any other defensive lineman in the Southwest Conference. An All-America in 1960, he became the Cowboys' first draft choice in 1961.

"Lilly was just what he appeared to

Lilly in his college All-Star uniform in 1961.

be—a big old country boy," said Gil Brandt, the Cowboy official who signed him. "I'll never forget putting him on the plane for the College All-Star game that summer. I suddenly looked down and realized Lilly didn't have on any socks."

The TCU publicity director, Jim Brock, attended the All-Star game and sought out coach Otto Graham to see how Lilly was doing.

"He's one of our biggest disappointments," said Graham.

"I couldn't believe it," Brock recalled later. "Then I learned that Graham had been trying to force Lilly to play *offense.*

That's like asking Raquel Welch to play boy."

The Cowboys made a similar mistake with Lilly, playing him out of position for two and a half years. Until midway through the 1963 season he played defensive end. When he moved to tackle he suddenly changed from a merely competent player to a great one. A year later, in his first full season at the position, Lilly made All-Pro.

Coach Landry explained the switch: "Bob is the type of boy who needs more freedom. An end has more responsibility in containing plays. A tackle can just go for the ball. Because of his great recovery ability Bob can afford to charge straight in and not worry about a definite responsibility. He's sort of a rover—not completely, because he still has a definite responsibility on certain plays. But we've been able to turn him loose pretty well and set the rest of our defense so that his area is covered."

The Cowboy coaches went over the films at the end of the 1964 season and found that Lilly was even more effective than they had suspected. Landry reported, almost in disbelief, "Lilly *always* broke his first block, and usually his second and his third, all season long. There is no single man in football who can contain him."

The better Lilly got, the more he was double-teamed and triple-teamed—and the more he was held. But he was so quick off the ball, and so intent on crashing through to bring down a quarterback or runner, that he wasn't always aware of the holding until he looked at the films after the game.

"Ninety percent of the guys hold," he said. "Some of the guys will just

Lilly has broken another block and gotten to Chicago ball-carrier Charlie Bivins in a 1964 game.

reach out and grab you under the shoulder pads. Some won't hold until you start to beat them on a pass rush. On a run, when you move laterally and they can't block you, then they just tackle you around the legs or grab wherever they can."

But he never used offensive holding as an excuse for a poor day: "That's part of the game if the refs don't call it. And they usually only call a guy for holding once a game. We've just got to overcome it."

As he got older, Lilly developed a

technique to stop the holding: he took to slapping a padded hand over an opponent's helmet ear-hole. He found that the shock would often "ring the player's bell" and cause him to lose his concentration. The player might even forget to hold.

But Lilly still couldn't bring himself to retaliate against holders as brutally as some defenders did. "I understand the holding," he said. "The guard knows there are only two ways for you to go around him. If he guesses wrong with you, he's got to do something, or his quarterback wouldn't live long."

Even coach Ernie Stautner felt a bit sorry for the guards who were assigned to stop Lilly. "He's got absolutely great quickness," said Ernie. "The people who play against him try to get set for his quickness. They think they know what to expect from studying films or even from playing against him before. But then they go up against him—and most of the time Bob's by them and into the backfield before they can get off the dime."

Still, for all his individual greatness, Bob Lilly was frustrated for ten years in the National Football League. The Cowboys came so close to a championship so many times in that period, only to lose out. The Cowboys compiled their best won-lost record up to then, 12–2 in 1968, but were defeated in the first round of the playoffs.

"I guarantee you, the guys who have been on this club awhile are tired of hearing and reading how the Cowboys have so many great athletes, so much finesse, so much imagination, so much speed," Lilly said. "One thing we don't have is the deepest respect of every rival,

because we've let some of them off the hook in the past. This has led to self-disgust, which is the sorriest feeling in the world. And the only way we're going to get rid of that feeling is to win the Super Bowl."

The next season the Cowboys again lost in the playoffs, but in 1970 they went all the way to the Super Bowl. Facing the Baltimore Colts, Dallas made many mistakes. With five seconds left on the clock and the score tied 13–13, the Colts set up a 32-yard field goal. Lilly tried to crash through and block the kick, but the ball cleared the crossbar, giving the Colts the victory.

Bob threw his helmet about 50 feet in the air. It came straight down and landed at his feet. He kicked it 20 yards and said to himself, "Well, we found another way to lose!"

"That reaction was stupid of me," Lilly said some months later. "But it took me a long time to get over that game."

In 1971 the Cowboys played their way into a second straight Super Bowl. In January of 1972 they faced the Miami Dolphins and beat them easily. And Bob Lilly was ecstatic.

"I think I'm beginning to like football even more," he said. "Victory in the Super Bowl brightens a man's entire existence and gives him a new eagerness. The satisfaction of knowing you are the best blots out all the disappointments and frustrations of the past. Now we're going to see if we can't win a few more Super Bowls."

In 1972, Bob Lilly played the whole season with a bad knee and a back injury that sent him to the hospital. Like many players, Lilly knew a lot about pain—from an assortment of football injuries. His wife Kitsey said football had also given Bob other unwanted gifts: "Ulcers . . . sleepless nights . . . depression after losses. When the Cowboys lose," she said, "he takes it like it's his fault and his feelings last about five days." She was eager to see Bob retire and spend more time with her and their three children.

Without a healthy Lilly, the Cowboys had no pass rush in 1972. They made the playoffs but lost the NFC championship game to the Redskins, and fans worried about how the Cowboys' defense could get along without Lilly. But Bob said it would be different when his injuries were healed, much different. He still had some Super Bowls to win before he could sleep.

Fingers taped loosely together and wrists bound, Lilly rests while the Cowboy offense plays.

Joe Namath

From the moment he entered pro football, quarterback Joe Namath of the New York Jets was the most exciting player in the game, both on the field and off. In the second game of the 1972 season against Baltimore he again showed what excitement he could generate on a Sunday afternoon.

The Jets had first played Baltimore in the 1969 Super Bowl and had scored a big upset victory. But since then, the Colts had won five in a row. They were particularly tough on a passer, having fine defensive backfield men who usually played a nearly perfect zone defense. The zone was supposed to make it impossible to throw the long pass successfully.

What was impossible for others was not impossible for Joe Namath. He passed for six touchdowns against the Colt zone—and four of them covered more than 65 yards. All told, his 15 completions gained 496 yards. It was the third-highest passing total in NFL history and quite likely the greatest overall performance ever by a passer.

Namath needed all those yards and touchdowns to assure the Jet victory because Baltimore kept coming back. Leading by only three points, 30–27, early in the fourth quarter, Namath saw the Colts send in a replacement at cornerback. Joe immediately sent tight end Rich Caster into the new man's zone, and the big Jet receiver raced past him to pull in a 79-yard touchdown pass.

John Unitas brought the Colts back to score again with six long minutes left,

again narrowing the Jets' lead to three points, 37–34.

"Waiting for the kickoff," Namath said later, "I was thinking about another long pass to Caster on the first play. But I wasn't sure if I should risk it, only three points ahead. Then I said to myself, 'If you ain't confident, you don't belong here.' So I decided to try to score again quick, because I knew there ain't no way we're going to use up the clock running the ball in that situation.

"I knew the Colts would be storming the walls. They blitzed on the first play, but I saw it coming and we picked it up. I knew Caster had to be one-on-one, so I just hustled the hell back there, set up, let the ball go, and it was just right."

That one covered 80 yards and locked up the win for New York, 44–34.

"We'd get those long drives going and score to close the gap," Unitas said afterward. "And then we'd go back to the bench, and in one play that guy would hit one for 80 yards and pull away again. It's kind of rough on you."

"You're laying deep back there because with Namath you're always afraid of the deep pass," added Baltimore's All-Pro safetyman Rich Volk. "But then he throws over your deep coverage anyway. I don't know—maybe I should have gambled more. But how can you gamble with a guy like Namath throwing? The whole thing was just amazing."

Namath agreed. "I was lucky," he said. "Some days you got it and some days you don't, and some days you can spit in a swinging jug. But if a good

Football's most exciting quarterback, the Jets' Joe Namath throws a pass against Baltimore.

quarterback has time, he can do well against a zone. All you do is send one or two people deep in one area and another deep underneath [between the linebackers and the defensive backs]— and that man underneath should be open. And there comes a time in every zone when part of it turns into man-to-man coverage. When you've got one man covering another man, you can throw long."

In the second Jet–Colt game of '72, Joe didn't have a great day. He completed only 5 of 16 passes in that one, and gave up three interceptions. Some of the incompletes weren't his fault. On one series of downs he fired three successive near-perfect passes. The first two were dropped, and the receiver of the third fell down as the ball arrived.

The Jets stayed close, however. And when the outcome depended on one play, Namath combined his skill with a little luck to provide a thrilling ending. With just over a minute left on the clock, the Jets were behind 20–17. They had the ball on their own 17-yard line. Namath decided in desperation to throw the ball up for grabs. He turned to swift little receiver Eddie Bell in the huddle and said, "Eddie, run your tail off."

Bell nodded and ran straight down the sideline. But he couldn't get beyond Colt cornerback Charlie Stukes or safetyman Jerry Logan. Namath threw the ball nearly 60 yards in the air, but Bell was still double-covered. The ball hit Stukes in the hand—then bounced into Bell's hands. Eddie raced into the end zone to bring the Jets a 24–20 victory.

"I'm supposed to do the job," Namath said with a smile afterward. "I get paid for it. It's cut and dried."

Prior to the 1972 season Joe had signed a two-year contract that indeed paid him well: about $250,000 per season. But his belief in his quarterbacking went well beyond his enormous salary.

"I'm convinced that I'm better than anybody else," he said. "I've been convinced of that for quite a while. Out there playing, I get annoyed at myself for doing something wrong. Sometimes I tell myself, 'You ain't too good,' and that helps me play better. Because then I tell myself, 'You're the best, damn it—do it right!' "

His cocky attitude and his lively lifestyle off the field didn't make Joe a favorite with every sports fan. In fact, at one point in his career he seemed to represent everything that older people thought was wrong with the younger generation. But personality aside, few

Namath smiles slyly to himself.

could disagree that "Broadway Joe" was one of the most spectacularly talented athletes in the game.

The youngest of four sons of a Hungarian steel worker, Joe Willie Namath grew up on the wrong side of the steel mill in Beaver Falls, Pennsylvania. In high school he was the high scorer and leading play-maker on the basketball team and such a hot prospect in baseball that he was offered a major league contract. As an all-star quarterback, he was also offered many college football scholarships.

Joe wanted to go to the University of Maryland or Notre Dame. But his scores on the college entrance exams kept him from qualifying at either. His third choice, Alabama, welcomed him.

94

On the football field at Alabama, Joe outshone every college quarterback of his time. In three years he passed for 3,055 yards and 29 touchdowns and helped Alabama to a national championship during his senior year.

Namath also had his share of trouble, though. He was suspended from the team by coach Bear Bryant for breaking training rules. Then during his senior year he received his first serious injury. Until that time, Joe had been a great running quarterback as well as a great passer. Then one game he was running a roll-out when his knee suddenly collapsed. He finished the game and virtually destroyed a ligament in the process. At season's end he underwent the first of many knee operations. Doctors said that Joe's trouble was related to a knee injury he had suffered when he was ten years old.

Despite the bad knee, Namath was far and away the outstanding quarterback in the country. The Jets of the American Football League and the St. Louis Cardinals of the NFL drafted him. The Jets were then a sad collection of second-rate players in a shaky new league. Owner Sonny Werblin, who had made a fortune in show business, knew that the team and the league

As quarterback at Alabama, Namath (12) runs with the ball in the 1963 Orange Bowl. Before his knee injuries, Namath could run almost as well as he could pass.

needed a big attraction. He settled on Joe and offered him a three-year contract worth $427,000. Joe accepted.

"I don't know how to define star quality," said Werblin, "but Joe Namath has it. It's something Joe will always have. When he walks into a room, he changes it."

Joe also changed the fortunes of the Jets. Their games suddenly became sell-out attractions in New York. And despite continuing problems with his knees, Namath became an immediate star on and off the field. He moved into a lavish bachelor apartment and escorted beautiful girls around town during the week. On Sundays he threw touchdown passes—a total of 18 during his rookie year.

Namath didn't forget his family, however. One of the first things he did with his bonus money was buy a new house for his mother. He wrote in his autobiography, "When I was growing up, my mother was a maid in Patterson Heights, the fancy section of Beaver Falls. At night, she'd stay up late, cutting down my brothers' old baseball and football uniforms to fit me. Now my mother lives in Patterson Heights."

In 1966, Joe threw 19 touchdown passes and threw for more than 3,300 yards. During the offseason he had another knee operation, but he came back in 1967 to become the first pro quarterback to pass for more than 4,000 yards in a season. He had a tremendous arm, the quickest release in football and the ability to read defenses instinctively right from the beginning. He had some things to learn, of course, but he learned quickly.

Despite Joe's passing records, the Jets had only an 8–5–1 record in 1967, and they missed qualifying for the AFL championship game. The next year, after his third knee operation, Namath began passing less. The Jets—with a much-improved defense and running game—won more. Joe threw for 3,147 yards, still an exceptional total. The Jets took the AFL Eastern Division title, then the AFL championship and earned the chance to meet the NFL champs, the Baltimore Colts, in the Super Bowl.

The Colts were rated 17-point favorites over the Jets, primarily because AFL teams had been slaughtered in the two earlier Super Bowls. "Seventeen-point underdogs?" said Namath. "That's silly. We're going to win. Bet on it."

Those who did collected. Joe Willie led the Jets to a 16–7 upset victory over Baltimore, passing for one touchdown and directing a cool, very controlled attack.

The Jet defense and numerous injuries conspired to defeat the Jets in 1969, and early the following year Namath broke his right wrist. Without him, the Jets were lost. The wrist healed in 1971, and Joe was anxious to play football again. But in an exhibition game against the Lions he had a pass intercepted and ran—despite his bad knees—to make the tackle. He was hit with a crushing block which re-injured one of his knees, and he was lost for most of the season. Once again the Jets were no threat without him.

"With him we're a 75 percent better football team," said veteran defensive end Gerry Philbin. "It's a fact of life. We can't do anything without him."

Namath got the Jets off to a fine start in 1972, but even the man called "a per-

In the 1969 Super Bowl against Baltimore, hero Namath hands off to running back Matt Snell.

fect passer" by coach Vince Lombardi could not do it all alone. The defense suffered some crucial injuries, then the Jets' top running backs got hurt and the team once again collapsed. Namath tried to do it all with his arm—which passed for over 400 yards in two games and for over 300 yards in three others. It wasn't enough. But Joe was not discouraged. He had bad knees that could cripple him permanently if he kept playing, and he was already rich and famous. But he kept playing.

"Football is a humbling game and even humiliating at times," Namath explained. "But it teaches you discipline and dedication, and there's a lot of competitive spirit. You can't cheat anybody out there. Football has been great for me."

John Niland

Dallas lineman John Niland on the move.

The Green Bay Packers were celebrating in their locker room after their 1967 NFL championship game victory over Dallas. Their coach, Vince Lombardi, was retiring, and they had helped him go out on a winning note. Some of the other Packer stars were nearing retire-

ment. One of the oldest, defensive tackle Henry Jordan, had finished celebrating and had begun peeling the dirty adhesive tape off his aching body. Then a stranger appeared in the locker room. Cowboy guard John Niland, who was in his second NFL season, had walked in and was tapping Henry on the shoulder.

"Mr. Jordan," he said, "I'm John Niland. I just want to tell you how much I enjoyed playing against you today."

Astonished, the balding veteran looked up at the freshly showered youngster, and said, "Why, John, thank you so much. You had to give us old geezers one more chance to win. You're a fine player, and someday soon you'll have your day."

John Niland would indeed go on to make All-Pro and help the Cowboys become champions.

Off the field, he was a very unusual human being. When Niland was playing football at the University of Iowa, for example, he met a six-year-old boy who had muscular dystrophy. John asked the youngster to visit the Hawkeyes' spring football practice. The boy did so and loved it.

"We quickly became very good friends," said John. "The doctors said the boy was going to die, and I wanted to do something for his family. They were kinda shy and suggested I just continue to be friends with their son. But I found out his older sister wanted to go to college and was having trouble because the family had no money. So I used some of the bonus money I got when I signed with the Cowboys in 1966 and set up a scholarship fund for her, stipulating that she maintain a B average as an incentive."

Two years later Niland decided he wanted to do more than that. He had begun making a good deal of money in the offseason as a speaker, getting paid from $50 to $500 per speech. He realized that he could afford to help needy students from his old high school who wanted to go on to college. He used his speaking fees to begin the John Niland Scholarship fund at Amityville High School in Amityville, New York. Two deserving youngsters received help from the fund every year.

"I gave each of them $500 to start and told them I would sponsor them as long as they needed money," said John.

"I have no criteria for these scholarships. The only thing I require is that the boy or girl—and they don't have to be involved in athletics—be deserving in the judgment of the athletic department, which administers the fund. It's just my small way of paying back. Football has been good to me, so I'd like to pay back a little of the good somehow."

John Niland knew what it was to need money, because he never had much himself as a youngster. "I was adopted," he said, "and my parents were very good to me, but we didn't have much. I began working at age eleven, first at a gas station, then at Al's Delicatessen. At Al's it was good experience—and really good eating."

He earned 50 cents an hour and all he could eat—which was considerable.

99

Niland works out with weights, increasing his size and strength.

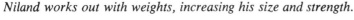

For six years John worked at Al's. And the extra food he was always eating played a part in his growing into a 230-pounder. His size and his athletic ability soon made him a star at Amityville High School. In his senior year the team was undefeated and John was named to the all-county squad at tackle. That won him a football scholarship to the University of Iowa, where he became an All-America guard and, incidentally, the school's heavyweight weight-lifting champion. The Cowboys drafted him in the first round—the first time they had ever selected an offensive lineman number one.

Weight lifting had increased John's neck to 20 inches, his chest to 50 inches and his weight to 245 pounds. But the 6-foot-3 Niland retained all of his speed and quickness, which combined with his strength to make him an amazing physical specimen. Still, as with most rookies, John found his first season as a pro was primarily a time for learning. He had realized just how much he had to learn during the College All-Star Game. That was when he first encountered the great Packer defensive tackle Henry Jordan.

"I had a no-hitter in that one," John admitted later. "I never blocked Henry once, I don't think. Well, I did the famous 'look-out' block. You lunge at your man and holler to your quarterback, 'look out!' Henry was a very smart football player."

But John didn't at all mind playing only part time in 1966. A year later he was a starter and helped Dallas into the NFL title game against Green Bay, where he met Henry Jordan once again. Within two years Niland made his first appearance on the All-Pro team. The Cowboys were up near the top every year, but they kept losing the crucial postseason playoff games. Then in 1970 they went all the way to the Super Bowl, but lost in a poorly played game, 16–13.

But the 1971 Cowboys were stronger than ever. When they met the Miami Dolphins in Super Bowl VI, Niland said in the operatic baritone that served him so well in speaking engagements: "I am very confident we'll win. The Dolphins have a very good defense—but we have a very good offensive team. And I think we'll execute very well. I think I can do things against Bob Heinz [the defensive tackle he would be facing] that will be very effective. I feel very confident attacking the man."

"Attacking" was an accurate description of how John Niland played football. In the 1972 Super Bowl game Heinz managed to get around John twice on passing plays, but otherwise he was tied up or knocked down all afternoon. Heinz was not the only man Niland hit, and the blocks John made on Dolphin middle linebacker Nick Buoniconti were the ones the fans noticed most. Buoniconti was the key to the Miami defense, and Niland was assigned to block him away from Cowboy running plays up the middle. The Cowboys ran and ran and ran, winning by a decisive 24–3.

"I know people usually look for me to lead our sweeps," John said afterward in the victors' dressing room. "But in this game our blocking assignments were different. We knew Miami and Buoniconti would be looking for us to run outside a lot, so we faked going outside and our ball-carriers cut back up the middle.

"Buoniconti's not that big for a mid-

As Calvin Hill (35) carries the ball, Niland (76) helps clear the way in a game against St. Louis.

dle linebacker, and he depends on his ability to read plays quickly. He would take the first fake and go out with the flow. Once he was out there, our ball-carriers would cut back against the flow, and he was easy to block."

John's right hand swept out, gesturing at his colleagues dressing nearby. "The offensive line—that's where the game was won," he said. "And we all made great blocks at one time or another."

Niland took pride in his position. Like many youngsters, when he first started playing football he wanted to play quarterback or offensive end, where

the glory lay. But he settled for what he could do exceptionally well, even at the beginning, which was block people. And he learned to love it.

"Most people don't realize what an exciting game it is in the line," he said. "That's where the action is. That's where you hit and get hit every time the ball is snapped. You hit a guy full speed 60 or 70 times a game—that's football. I like to knock people on their butts. It's exciting to me to make a block, to get the feel of driving into a guy, the contact, and then feeling him going back.

"A guard has the most difficult job in the line. He's at the point of attack 99 percent of the time, pulling, leading the play, trapping, zone blocking. A quarterback can make the big plays. But if the offense is going to maintain any kind of momentum, it depends on the line—its experience, its quickness, its decisions at the snap. I don't carry the ball, so I can't physically move it down the field. But I can grab this team in my hands and move it. We all can. You have to grab the reins right there in the line."

Niland leads Cowboy running back Duane Thomas on a sweep—Niland's favorite play.

Niland's favorite play was the sweep. At the snap of the ball, he "pulled"— pivoting out of his set position and sprinting toward the sideline, leading the interference for the ball-carrier. When he turned upfield, the ball-carrier was racing along right behind him and John would smash into a defender to clear the runner's path.

There was a touch of the poet in John's words when he talked about his all-important role in the sweep play: "I like to get out of the dust bowl, out into the clean, fresh air. A sweep is like music to my ears. I envision the play, I feel the momentum of it. There's a certain rhythm in the play—pulling, the backs coming behind me, making my block, the play flowing through me. God, I do love my job."

Niland was perhaps the most conscientious offensive lineman in the league in preparing for a game. Every season he carried around with him, week after week, a thick folder that slowly grew even thicker. It contained all the Cowboy offensive game plans and John's own private scouting reports on every defensive tackle he had ever faced. He would continually update the information in his folder.

"A player's tendencies, the things that make him good, are the same year in and year out," said John. "Basically, a tackle can only do certain things: lead with a certain arm or a certain leg, take a certain stance. By constantly studying the guys I'm going up against, I'm ready for them. My study makes my job more interesting, too, because football can get boring when you play over 20 games a season. I study so much that the game itself can be an aftermath. But

I always feel that the most prepared ballplayer is the one who'll come out on top."

John also prepared well for life when his football career would end. In college he majored in finance and, after joining the Cowboys, took a job with a bank in Dallas. He soon rose from loan officer to vice president. He also had his own television show on Dallas station KDTV. But what he seemed to like most of all was traveling around speaking to youngsters, trying to get them to channel their energies into worthwhile endeavors, rather than into destructive things like drugs.

"Most high school kids don't know what competition is," John said. "They can learn it from football. Now, some kids don't make the team, and they take to pot and drugs. That's sad. In a sense they've made another team— they're escaping from reality. Athletics is not the entire answer, but it is a help. If football players get involved with kids, the kids will probably stay away from drugs. Kids do relate to football."

Niland was the Cowboys' representative to the NFL Players' Association, and he got a number of his teammates involved in working with youngsters. He was also pleased that his wife Iree did a lot of volunteer work with kids. And he made another contribution to youth through the scholarship program that sent so many young people to college.

"I feel there are many John Nilands in high school today," said John. "I get my kicks on the football field, knocking guys on their tails. Kids today are looking for excitement. You put a kid in college and he might find the right kind of excitement—from books."

Alan Page

Twice a year the Minnesota Vikings and the Detroit Lions play each other in the struggle for the title in the NFC's Central Division, often called the NFL's "black-and-blue division." Both teams take such a gang-fight approach to football that it would surprise nobody if one day the teams ran onto the field carrying garbage can covers and lengths of chain.

The second Viking-Lion meeting in 1971 was typical, except for one thing.

Viking defensive tackle Alan Page—who was almost never called for penalties—was called for two successive personal fouls. First he was called for applying a head slap to a Lion guard beyond the point where such a blow is legal. In a rare emotional display, Alan raged at the referee, saying the blow had occurred on the first step of his charge and was therefore perfectly within the rules. The referee said Page had clapped

As Detroit quarterback Greg Landry gets ready to throw, he faces ferocious Alan Page.

his opponent's helmet on the *second* step, and walked off a 15-yard penalty.

On the next play Page, who was still upset, immediately burst past his blocker. But he ran into the fullback, who was protecting the passer. Alan finally fought through that block and rammed into the Lion quarterback—an instant after he'd gotten off his pass. This time Page was called for roughing the passer, another 15-yard penalty.

Although Alan didn't protest this call, he was visibly upset. After all, what could be more frustrating for a defensive player than to advance the ball 30 yards for the opposition? But the Lions would have gladly returned those penalty yards if they had only known what was to follow. For on the next five plays, the 6-foot-3, 244-pound Page showed why he would become the first lineman ever voted Most Valuable Player in the National Football League.

On the first play Page blasted into the backfield so quickly that Lion blockers barely touched him, dropping quarterback Greg Landry for a nine-yard loss. Then he drove through the line and tackled ball-carrier Altie Taylor for a four-yard loss. On third down, he fired past his man, who desperately reached out and grabbed Page, committing a 15-yard holding penalty.

When third down was replayed, Page chased Landry out of the pocket and tackled him from behind after a two-yard gain. On fourth down, Page shot through the tight wall of blockers, leaped high in the air and blocked the punt. The ball skittered out of the end zone for a safety, giving the Vikings two points that helped them clinch another title.

As Alan walked off the field, head up, large brown eyes straight ahead, two of his partners in the great Viking defensive line hurried up on either side of him. Tackle Gary Larsen and end Carl Eller each threw an arm around Page as the hometown crowd stood in slack-jawed silence, awed by the individual performance they had just witnessed.

"I'd have to rank the Vikings among the best defenses in the last ten years," Lion coach Joe Schmidt said after the game. "The thing that makes them so effective is Carl Eller and Alan Page, particularly Page. When Page wants to come, he *comes*. There just aren't any more like him, anywhere."

"Alan Page is the most relentless player I've ever seen," said former Viking defensive coach Bob Hollway. But relentless—which the dictionary defines as "mercilessly hard or harsh"—was not the precise word to apply to Alan Page if there is any hint of "meanness" in it.

"You know, when Alan was at Notre Dame," his wife Lorraine once remarked, "the defensive coach, Johnny Ray, came up to me one time and said, 'What can we do about Alan? He's just not *mean* enough.'"

Certainly Page was relentless in the sense that he never let up in a game. As Viking defensive line coach Jack Patera pointed out: "I've never seen a player *go* as consistently as Page does. Where the ball goes, Alan goes. It doesn't matter if it's a 60-yard pass, he turns and chases it down. That's how he recovers so many fumbles way downfield. This kind of pursuit is something you try to instill in every player, condition him to do. But you can only improve a player's pursuit, you can't teach anyone to do it

Page catches 49er quarterback John Brodie.

the way Alan does. It's either in you or it isn't."

In 1971, the season he was voted the league's Most Valuable Player, Page made 109 tackles, assisted on 35 others, dropped quarterbacks for losses ten times and aided in two other "sackings."

But tackling a quarterback behind the line is not necessarily the most meaningful statistic in judging a defensive lineman's effectiveness. The Vikings kept another statistic—called "hurries"—that perhaps tells more about a pass rusher. When a defender forces a quarterback to hurry his throw, he is credited with a "hurry." Page had 42 in 1971. Forty-two times Alan put so much pressure on quarterbacks that they had to throw before they were set properly or before

their receiver got open. Thus "hurries" often cause interceptions. That's one reason the Vikings were so difficult to pass against after Page joined them.

Seeing Alan toweling off in a locker room, one might think the secret of his pass-rushing ability was his strength and power. Although he was actually rather light for a defensive tackle at 244 pounds, he seemed larger than life, every water-sprinkled muscle immense. It was obvious that he could have used the battering, brute-force techniques most linemen employ on every down— throwing a club-like forearm into the blocker's gut, using his hands to yank the guard aside with all the finesse of a street brawler. But these techniques, which are legal for the defenders, did not appeal to Page, who seldom even used the head slap. He relied almost entirely on quickness to get past his blocker. Alan fired out so swiftly on the snap of the ball that he was sometimes on his way into the enemy backfield before the guard could set himself to stop him.

"I rely on quickness to penetrate, and then I react to the ball," Alan said. "Mostly I just try to get off on the snap and beat my guy to a certain point. Once I've gotten a certain amount of depth, I know I've pretty well got him."

"Page embarrassed me," said Green Bay guard Bill Lueck after struggling to keep himself between Page and the Packer offensive backs throughout one long game. "He was never where he was supposed to be. He just drove me crazy. I never saw anyone play tackle the way he does."

After another game, Chicago quarterback Bobby Douglass shook his head

A split-second after the ball is snapped, Page is on his way into the Chicago Bear backfield.

and said, "Page is in your backfield before you are."

Page's eye-blurring quickness forced many guards—even the better ones—to grab him and hold on for their quarterback's dear life. Offensive holding is, of course, a 15-yard penalty. But officials don't always call the holding that goes on.

"A lot of guards hold a bunch," Page once said in the quiet way he spoke off the field. "In one game recently somebody ripped the name-tag off the back of my jersey, and there was no holding call. And one of the Bears tore my chin strap right in half—not off, *in half*—and there still was no penalty. When I was a rookie I couldn't understand why all the veterans were getting so angry about the holding. Maybe I wasn't worth holding then, I don't know. But it's gotten so bad since then that it really gets sickening at times. You have a tendency to get somewhat irate."

When most defensive linemen get angry over being held, they eventually take steps to put a stop to the clutching hands. These steps are often as far outside the rules as the holding itself. They include such measures as kicking, slugging and even biting. A penalty, they decide in their anger, is worth it if the holding ceases. What did Page do when the holding infuriated him? "I usually try to get the attention of the officials," Alan said coolly.

Although Alan Page was one of the most emotional football players ever—which is why he consistently performed with such relentless determination—he almost always kept his emotions under firm control. Unnecessary violence, he determined quite rightly, would only obstruct the job at hand.

"I have to use my emotion and not let it get in the way of making the correct play," he explained. "See, I start off a game already emotionally high, and the longer the game goes on, the higher I get. I don't show my emotions much, but inside me it's like a fire. With every play I get more involved, more intense. Everything that happens in a game pulls me in more and more—until my concentration is total. The game is absolutely all I can think of.

"Then, all of a sudden, *bang,* the game is over and I'm sitting in the locker room. There are people around and I'm supposed to relate to them. It's really a strange feeling. It's hard to adjust back to reality—to have to be a person again."

Alan's experiences as a youth helped mold him into the thoughtful, serious, self-contained man he became. He grew up in Canton, Ohio, a town famous for football and the site of the Pro Football

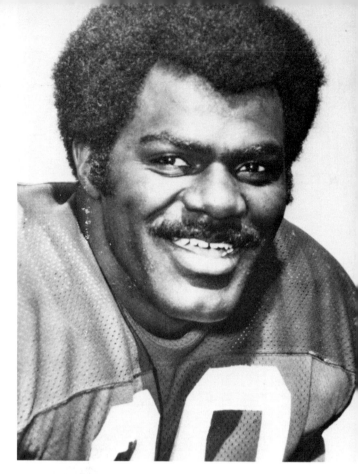

Alan Page: first defensive lineman to be MVP.

Hall of Fame. When Alan was a junior in high school his dad built a house twelve miles away in East Canton because Mrs. Page wanted to live in the country.

Shortly afterward, when Alan was 14, his mother died suddenly while undergoing surgery. The family was pulled close by the tragedy, but it also forced a certain independence on Alan. His two older sisters became the women of the house, and he followed his older brother to Central Catholic High School and the football team. Coach Murray Warmath, who tried to recruit Page for his University of Minnesota team, later said, "Alan Page was the best high school football player I've ever seen."

From among many college scholarship offers, Alan chose Notre Dame. He majored in political science, excelling in his classwork as well as in football. In

Page's first varsity season Notre Dame hired the very successful college coach Ara Parseghian to rebuild the Fighting Irish team, which had been suffering through bad times for years. Aided by Page and a host of other young stars, Parseghian made Notre Dame a big winner again. Alan made All-America and became a first-round draft choice of the Vikings.

During the first three games of the 1967 season, rookie Page got to play only fill-in roles. He immediately displayed his relentless style, and by his fourth game coach Bud Grant had made him a starter. For several weeks Alan alternately made fine plays and bad ones. Then, during a 10–10 tie with a tough Detroit team, Page was credited with six tackles and five assists—and he caused four Detroit fumbles. He was named the league's Defensive Player of the Week by the Associated Press, and within two seasons he became a regular member of the All-Pro team. By the end of his fifth season in the NFL, Page was such an exceptional defensive tackle that sportswriters and coaches were already predicting that he would one day be a member of the Pro Football Hall of Fame.

Alan wasn't thinking about that possibility, though. A warm, quiet family man, his primary interest was his wife Lorraine, their two daughters and their adopted son. Next came football, and close behind that came his passion for automobile racing.

"I've been interested in cars as long as I can remember," Page explained. And after the 1971 season Alan finally realized his long-time dream by becoming an offseason drag racer. He bought a 300-horsepower Dodge Charger and entered a race in Coon Rapids, Minnesota. Then he surprised the experts, not only winning his first professional race, but setting a new national record time in his class. Alan Page, it seemed, was as relentless on a drag strip as he was on a football field.

Page (88) and a teammate bring down Green Bay receiver John Hilton and jar the ball loose.

Jim Plunkett

110

In a 1971 exhibition game against the Atlanta Falcons, rookie quarterback Jim Plunkett called a play in the huddle, clapped his hands and broke out of the huddle. So did rookie receiver Randy Vataha. The rest of the New England Patriots just stood there, staring at the two first-year men who had played college football together at Stanford.

"Suddenly I realized what I'd done," Plunkett recalled later. "I'd called a Stanford play. The rest of the team thought I'd gone crazy. But it was a very hot day, I'd just been hit hard a few times and I was a little dingy. When I realized what I'd done, I felt like crawling away. It was just a normal rookie mistake, though."

Plunkett went on to make his share of normal rookie mistakes in his first NFL season. But he also completed almost 50 percent of his passes and had less than five percent of them intercepted. And he threw 19 touchdown passes for one of the worst teams in the league. As rookies, Joe Namath and Fran Tarkenton each threw 18, Bob Griese 15, Johnny Unitas 9, and Terry Bradshaw only 6.

"Plunkett is going to be a superstar," announced veteran pass rusher Deacon Jones the first time he saw him play. "And he'll get there faster than any quarterback who has come up in my time."

How had the 6-foot-3, 215-pound Plunkett been able to do well in his very first year when so many other rookie quarterbacks with great potential had failed miserably? "Because those other kids never had any pressure on them until they came to the pros," answered Patriot general manager Upton Bell. "This guy Plunkett has had pressure on him all his life."

Jim Plunkett was the son of parents who were blind, and he was also a member of a minority group. Born December 5, 1947, in San Jose, California, he was an American of Mexican descent. Jim went to work as soon as he was big enough to sling a bundle of newspapers over his shoulder. He pumped gas when he was twelve. His family never starved, but it needed all the help it could get—even from a grade-schooler.

Jim also began playing football early. He was a guard in grade school and began as a defensive end in high school. But by that time he was big for his age and had a strong throwing arm. A coach saw him throw a few passes in practice one day, and the next day Jim was a quarterback. He was also a top student. From among a great many college scholarship offers, he chose nearby Stanford first "because I wanted to stay close to home," and second "because I heard so much about Stanford's fine academic record."

When he entered the university in 1966, a physical examination revealed a tumor on his neck. Radioactive iodine tests indicated the tumor was malignant. Jim faced removal of the tumor through surgery.

"I was scared," Jim recalled. "I said, 'No, I won't have it operated on.' My folks talked me into it."

Fortunately, despite the results of the iodine test, the tumor proved to be benign. But Plunkett tried to play football too soon after the surgery. "I didn't play well," he said. "In fact, I played crummy." Near the close of that season the freshman coach suggested that Jim might do better at defensive end.

"Give me time," said Plunkett. "See what you say next fall."

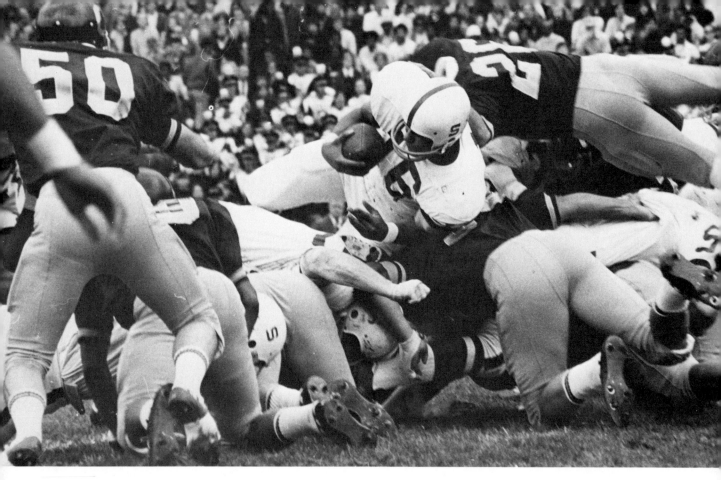

In the 1970 Rose Bowl, Stanford's Jim Plunkett tries a quarterback sneak against Ohio State.

In the fall he was throwing much better. But by then the coaches had decided to red-shirt him, let him sit out of varsity competition for a year. When his varsity career finally began in 1968, Plunkett was ready. He had a top sophomore receiver to work to in Randy Vataha, and an even better senior end in Gene Washington (who later went on to star for the 49ers).

The Indians had a powerful offense. But through Plunkett's three varsity seasons, the Stanford defense was inconsistent. Jim was fighting other problems, too. He injured his right knee on a run in his third game as a sophomore. He refused to have the damaged cartilage removed until season's end, but his play suffered. The next year Stanford was again mediocre. During the season Jim's father died of a heart attack, reminding Jim that the worst moments in a person's life seldom come on a football field.

Then in 1970, Jim led the Indians to a heroic season. Although they lost three regular-season games, Jim had some fantastic afternoons and the team won their conference championship, which meant a Rose Bowl meeting with Ohio State.

The Buckeyes had lost only one game in three years and were heavy favorites. Going into the fourth quarter Stanford trailed 14–10, but Plunkett was not discouraged. "We knew we could move the ball," he said later. "We were confident." He promptly completed a long pass to Ohio State's two-yard line to set up a touchdown. On the next series he hit Vataha with a scoring pass and Stanford went on to win, 27–17.

"Isn't that Plunkett something!" coach John Ralston said afterward. Experts decided he was the best college football player in the country, awarding him the Heisman Trophy to prove it.

"He's the best quarterback prospect since Joe Namath," said John Mazur, coach of the Patriots. The Pats had had the worst record in the NFL in 1970, so they got first choice in the college draft. Their pick: Plunkett.

Jim went off to the College All-Star game thinking that he wouldn't play much once he reported to the Patriots. They already had a pair of veteran quarterbacks in Joe Kapp and Mike Taliaferro. Having to play in the All-Star game didn't help either.

"I had to do all the throwing in practice," Plunkett said afterward. "By the time I got to the Patriot camp, I had a dead arm."

But events were pushing Jim toward the spotlight. First-string quarterback Joe Kapp never signed a contract with the Pats. Taliaferro, the second-stringer, wasn't looking good. The team lost five of six exhibition games, and when the regular season opened, Jim was the starting quarterback.

After the first half of the season opener against a tough Oakland Raider team, Boston had given up only two field goals and trailed 6–0. "I had called only four passes, everything else was basic power stuff," said Jim. "But our defense held them to six points and they were making a lot of mistakes. In the second half we made an adjustment that put Ron Sellers one-on-one against Nemiah Wilson—and there's nobody who can cover Sellers one-on-one."

Plunkett hit Sellers for one touchdown. The Raiders adjusted their defenses, and then Jim hit end Roland Moss on another scoring pass. The Patriots finally upset the Raiders 20–6.

New England lost its next three games, to Detroit, Baltimore and Miami, scoring only 13 points to their opponents' 98. In a downpour the following week against the Jets, who were without the injured Joe Namath, Plunkett did not play particularly well. Nevertheless, the Patriots won, 20–0.

Then three of the best teams in the league, the Dolphins, Cowboys and 49ers, tore up the Patriots. Plunkett was not disheartened, but neither was he sure of himself.

"I would call a play," he said, "and then look at center John Morris to see if he thought it would work. Sometimes he would shake his head and tell me, 'That play won't work because of the way they're pinch-blocking.' So I'd call another play. What really bothered me was when I'd call a play and say, 'Flanker 40 . . . uh, no, I mean Flanker 30.' When you do that too often you worry that you're losing the team's confidence.

"In the first half of the season I was calling the same play a lot: 36 Power. It's an off-tackle play, and the blocking is always the same in any situation. I worried so much about my play selection, I think it detracted from my throwing. I wasn't setting up right. I wasn't throwing as well as I can. In the second half of the season, as I got more confidence in my play selection, I was throwing better."

One thing that helped Plunkett learn his job was that coach Mazur let him call nearly all his own plays. On a big

Young Jim Plunkett calls signals for the Patriots during his amazingly successful rookie year.

third down or in a particularly complex situation, the coach would send in a play. Even then, though, Plunkett could change it if he felt something else would go better. Jim was learning quickly despite the 2–6 early season record.

In game nine Plunkett threw four scoring passes against the Bills, as the Pats won 38–33. "That was when I began to think I was getting to be a half-decent pro quarterback," Jim said.

Then the Browns beat the Patriots and, in a second game against Buffalo, the Bills won 27–10 as Plunkett gave up four interceptions. His confidence in his passing plunged. If he could be beaten by the last-place Bills, what would happen against powerful Miami?

Jim started off against the Dolphins by calling eight straight passing plays. He went on to complete 16 of 23, and the Patriots beat the Dolphins, 34–13, picking up their second big upset of the year.

After a 13–6 loss to the Jets in which an unusual Jet defense fooled Plunkett, he played his headiest game of the year in the season's finale. Leading the Colts 14–10 with a third and 12 and only minutes left on the clock, Jim did not call a safe run. He called a long pass to Vataha. Center John Morris' face

As running back Carl Garrett blocks, Plunkett gets set to throw.

showed disbelief in the huddle and Plunkett considered changing his call. But Jim took the risk to avoid punting. He knew what dangerous Johnny Unitas could do in the closing minutes of a ball game.

Jim faked a hand-off into the line, which held the Colt safetyman momentarily and allowed Vataha to break open down the sideline. Then Jim faded and snapped the ball out to him on a long, hard line. Vataha scored what proved to be the winning touchdown as the Pats won 21–17.

"When Kapp walked out of camp," said John Mazur, "there was a leader-ship vacuum. This kid came along, a Heisman Trophy winner—and you know how many of them have failed in pro football—but he never complained. He took his beatings and he was simply saying, 'I am a young quarterback, I am learning.' The guys began to respect him. That was the beginning of the making of Jim Plunkett."

The young quarterback and many others expected his second season to be even better. Certainly Jim had a fine exhibition season. He shocked the NFL by leading the Patriots to upset victories over Atlanta and Washington when the season opened. But then the Patriots abruptly fell apart, losing to Cincinnati 31–7, to Buffalo 38–14, and so on through a disheartening year.

"We're not coming up with the big plays like we did last year," Jim lamented. "We're moving the ball, but we're not scoring. We have key breakdowns in key situations. I throw an interception, we fumble the ball away or someone misses a block. And the defense isn't playing well either."

One problem was minor but nagging injuries to Plunkett. He started off with a sore arm, then had badly bruised ribs, then banged up his passing shoulder, then pulled a muscle in his leg.

But the real problem, of course, was the Patriots. Coach John Mazur was fired at midseason, end Ron Sellers was traded, and halfback Carl Garrett—the team's top running back—was suspended. Getting little help from his friends, Plunkett completed only 47.6 percent of his passes in '72. His yardage total—2,196—wasn't bad, but his interception total of 25 certainly was.

Nevertheless, the Patriots' inglorious record assured them of some high draft picks with which to rebuild. New England already had the perfect man to build around. As Los Angeles Ram scout and former star quarterback Bob Waterfield said, "If I was going to start a pro team tomorrow and could choose any young quarterback, I'd take Jim Plunkett."

"He's going to be great," said Redskin cornerback Pat Fischer.

Considering what Jim Plunkett had been through in his early life, one thing seemed certain—he wouldn't give up easily.

When his passing protection breaks down, big, strong Plunkett runs with the ball himself.

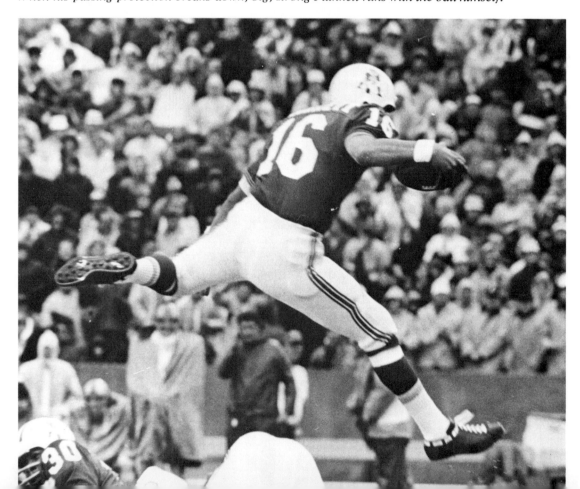

Tim Rossovich

Linebacker Tim Rossovich twists like a pretzel trying to tackle Oakland's Cas Banaszak.

In an exhibition game on the night of August 19, 1972, Charger middle linebacker Tim Rossovich saw that the San Francisco 49er ball-carrier would be banging across the line off tackle. Rossovich moved to his left toward the runner, but 49er center Forrest Blue fired out low at Rossovich's legs to cut him off. Tim was not in top condition—he had come to the Chargers only two weeks earlier after a lengthy salary dispute with his old team, the Eagles.

Rossovich reacted too slowly to fend off the massive center. As Blue drove into Tim's right knee, it buckled, tearing the cartilage and damaging the ligaments. He was operated on the next day, and doctors said he was finished for the season.

Of course, the Charger physicians didn't know Rossovich very well. Two years earlier, in an exhibition game with the Eagles, he was hit and felt something snap in his left ankle. He kept chasing the ball-carrier until he noticed that he was running on the *top* of his foot. At halftime he got a cortisone shot and had the ankle taped so that the sole of his foot would stay on the ground. Then he played the second half.

Tim had torn the tendon in his ankle and partially ruptured the muscle. The Eagle doctor told him he needed immediate surgery, which would sideline him six weeks. Rossovich punched a steel locker and yelled, "No!" He was determined to try and play the next game: if he performed without hurting the team, he would wait till season's end for the operation. Amazingly, he managed to play the entire season on the painful, tendonless ankle. The muscle on the outside of the ankle developed so well that it was able to support him.

"I've never really minded pain," Rossovich explained later. "You can't let injuries bother you in football."

Tim didn't let the knee injury with the Chargers bother him all that much, either. Before the ninth game of the 1972 season, the announcer in San Diego intoned: "Starting at middle linebacker, number 82, Tim Rossovich."

He played only the first half, but he seemed as good as ever. He made two unassisted tackles, assisted on three others and knocked down two passes. At least twice he forced the Browns' quarterback to throw to a secondary receiver by covering Cleveland running backs so well on pass patterns. Rossovich played just about as he always had —dashing all over the field with a kind of mad intensity.

"I'm hyperactive," he once said. "I've always gotta be doing something, I can't just be lying around. When I do, I feel like I'm starting to rust."

Rossovich stood 6-foot-4 and usually started a season weighing between 230 and 240 pounds. But by the end of the schedule he would be down to around 200 pounds. His hyperactivity made it hard to keep his playing weight no matter how much food he consumed. It also allowed him to bounce back from injuries that would have crippled normal people. But then, no one ever accused Tim Rossovich of being normal. The hyperactivity that helped make him a great football player, also led to some bizarre and amusing behavior off the field.

In 1972, after his leg was put in a cast, Rossovich—apparently fearful that

Shaggy, mustachioed Rossovich poses for a training photo in 1971 . . .

he would start to rust if he didn't do something—decided one day to go swimming, much to the disadvantage of the cast. Another day he was seen hobbling nonchalantly along the third-floor ledge of a house. Then one afternoon Tim pulled up to a Charger practice. His car suddenly stopped dead, the door flew open and Tim fell, stiff as a corpse, onto the ground.

"They're just spontaneous things," said Tim. "I just like to have fun. I've always liked to have fun."

The possibilities for having fun were even an important consideration to Rossovich when he was selecting a college to attend. After an outstanding career as a tight end, linebacker and fullback at St. Francis High School in Palo Alto,

... but in October he hides his face with a towel after the coach ordered mustaches shaved off.

California, he received more than 50 college scholarship offers. He visited his two top choices, Notre Dame and Southern California.

"At Notre Dame they took me to a movie. At USC they took me to a party," Tim said. "I chose USC."

There he became an immediate sensation for his play on the freshman team and for his stunts at parties. But one of his first party stunts almost ended in tragedy. Tim went to the affair after cutting his arm at practice. Soon he was doing fully-clothed, fancy dives into a fish pond that was filled with stagnant water. In a short while his arm ballooned, infected by the filthy water. Friends took him to the USC health center, and he was put to bed.

But late that night the infection shot up to his brain, and Tim went berserk. He turned over his bed and tore up his room. Campus police wrestled him into a strait jacket, but he ripped it off. Finally he collapsed into a coma. For four days he lay unconscious, and doctors feared he would die.

"Then I woke up feeling fine," he said later, "though I don't remember anything I did. The doctors said I couldn't play football that season, because they were afraid of what might happen if I got hit in the head. So every day when the team reported to practice, I'd run into the dressing room and bang my head into a locker door. 'Look, coach,' I'd yell, 'I feel fine!' After two months of this all the lockers were bent. But I got to play the last two games of the season."

The next three years were full of football heroics as Rossovich made All-America at defensive end and co-captained the 1967 national champion-

119

ship team at Southern Cal. These years were equally full of wild and wacky stunts by Rossovich, as he led his fraternity brothers in such pleasurable activities as wrecking old cars.

"We'd drive out in the hills and see who could roll over the most times," Tim recalled. "And we used to race around the parking lot and crash into the walls. It didn't hurt anything, just wrinkled the cars a little."

Rossovich once drove his Triumph convertible up a dozen steps into his fraternity house, made a left into the living room, ran over a coffee table, spun into the dining room and skidded to a halt.

"I thought I did pretty well, missing all that furniture except for one coffee table," he said. "But everyone jumped up from their tables and dumped their food into my car. I had to back down the steps and wash out the car with a fire hose."

Another of Tim's jokes was the talk of USC for weeks. "A bird flew into the frat house window one day," Tim said, "and I caught it. Everyone else was in the dining room eating lunch. So I put the bird in my mouth, walked into the dining room, stopped at a table and tapped on a glass for attention. When everyone looked at me, I spread my arms as if to speak, opened my mouth—and the bird flew out."

Not everyone laughed at Tim's pranks. Tim said one year he had to pay nearly $2,000 to repair the damage he had done to the frat house. Luckily he made good money working as an extra on television shows during the summers. After summoning Rossovich to his office three times for disciplinary

reasons, the dean of men at Southern Cal finally asked to see Tim's parents.

"He suggested to my parents that I see a psychiatrist," Tim recalled. "My parents weren't happy about it, but my antics were nothing new to them. They'd raised me and knew I had always been kind of wild and crazy. In fact, it might be true—maybe I should see a psychiatrist."

Tim's strange behavior off the field did not prevent him from being the Philadelphia Eagles' top pick in the pro draft of 1968. He had an excellent year at defensive end as a rookie and made the Pro Bowl squad in his second season. He was a vicious tackler, was extremely quick and had great range—perfect middle linebacker skills. After five games in the 1970 season he was switched to middle backer. Nothing could have made him happier.

"Deep down," he said, "I had always wanted to play there, to be right in the middle of everything. Middle linebacker really turns me on. I have the whole, total picture before me on every play. I can see and feel everything, run all over the field and hit people. I can express myself more."

In only nine games Rossovich so impressed Jimmy Carr, the Eagle defensive coach, that Carr said, "Tim rates right up among the top four middle linebackers in the league right now. He's amazing. There's no telling how far he can go."

David Lloyd, the veteran middle linebacker who was replaced by Rossovich, had to give Tim credit. "His greatest asset is his destroying attitude," Lloyd said.

"That's something you've got to have

Although many thought Rossovich crazy, he usually got his man—this time Cowboy Calvin Hill.

to play anyplace on defense," said Tim. "It sounds bad, but it's pretty satisfying to hit somebody, to feel him grunt, bounce him off the ground and see his eyes rolling around. That guy's gonna be looking out for you the next time."

Rossovich played a very physical game, but he also lashed out at opponents with his mouth. He seldom remembered what he yelled in the heat of battle, but NFL films caught his words in one game against Pittsburgh. "I love you, man," he hollered at a Steeler player, "but I gotta wipe you out." Many of his other taunts were too salty to print.

Even as Rossovich was improving as a football player, he was continuing his antics off the field. He ate light bulbs, stuck pins into his arms and participated in contests to see who could open the most beer bottles with their teeth. Tim never lost. Although not all his teammates admired him, most had a favorite story about his outrageous pranks.

"Tim's image [as a crazy man] belies the seriousness with which he plays football," said Eagle linebacker coach Joe Moss. In 1971, Tim was in on 149 tackles—averaging over ten per game, a high mark indeed.

But apparently Tim's off-the-field style did not please the Eagle management. Despite his great season, he was offered no raise for 1972. Tim refused to report to training camp, and after a 16-day holdout he was traded to San Diego. Many people thought he would be thrilled to play in his home area on the West Coast. But when he was told of the trade and visited his Eagle teammates in training camp for the last time, there were tears in his eyes.

"I love those people in that dormitory," he said just before he drove away. "If I stayed with those guys any longer, I would've cried like a baby.

"People know I'm a goofball," said Tim Rossovich. "When I feel like doing something, I do it. I don't do anything to hurt anyone. But I enjoy all phases of life, particularly the unconventional. I don't want to die without having experienced everything I can. But I also want to be a great middle linebacker— and I'm going to be."

Rossovich (right) goes after Miami's Larry Csonka—and the football.

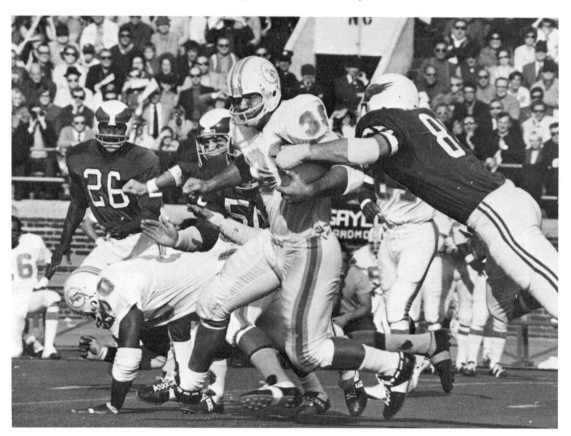

O. J. Simpson

In 1972 the Buffalo Bills were hit with the most incredible string of injuries in recent memory, particularly to the offensive line. The Bills were not a powerful team to begin with, and by midseason they had used eight different right guards, four centers, two left guards and three left tackles. It hardly seemed like a promising year for a Buffalo running back, who would have to depend on that revolving-door line for blocking. But O.J. Simpson didn't seem to mind.

First he made jokes about it. In the opening huddle of one game he looked around at the unfamiliar faces and asked, "Does everybody here know everybody else?"

Then he went on to become the top rusher in the National Football League, gaining 1,251 yards. It was a spectacu-

lar effort—especially while playing for a team with crippled linemen, a mediocre passing attack and a 4–9–1 record.

Simpson's great performance in 1972 fulfilled the promise he had shown as the top college running back in the country and the top draft choice of the Bills in 1969. But Buffalo was still a loser, and O.J. wasn't satisfied. "I've cried with these guys through the last few bad years," he said. "Now I want to drink champagne with them. I want to be around when we turn this team into a winner—it won't be long."

O.J., his brother and two sisters grew up in a black neighborhood in San Francisco. Their mother, a hospital worker, raised them, and she hoped O.J. would become a baseball player like his cousin, Ernie Banks of the Cubs. But O.J. was more interested in football and track at Galileo High School, where 70 percent of the students were of Oriental descent. As a 5-foot-10, 160-pound freshman, Simpson was the second-biggest player on the team. Coach Jack McBride put him on the line, "but only until I saw him run with the ball."

O.J. ran fast and tough, on and off the field. During his first two years in high school he was always in trouble for cutting classes, smoking and getting into fights. Twice he even was held overnight in juvenile hall for misbehaving. "If it hadn't been for football," he said later, "I guess I would have just quit school. I wasn't thinking about the future."

Then he met a girl named Marguerite Whitley, whom he later married, and he began thinking about his future. He started attending classes regularly and

became an all-city halfback in his senior year. But his scholastic record was so poor that no four-year college could accept him.

So O.J. enrolled at City College of San Francisco—and became the greatest junior-college runner in history. In his first season he averaged 9.9 yards per carry and scored 26 touchdowns in ten games. Although the entire City College offensive line graduated after that first season, O.J. came back to score 28 touchdowns his second year. By then he had grown to 6-foot-2 and weighed 215 pounds. He was big enough and strong enough to run over most defenders. But O.J. seldom had to. He easily zipped past tacklers on a pair of the quickest feet ever to slip into football cleats. He soon had an awesome reputation among his opponents.

"We all wore red-and-white helmets at CCSF," recalled a teammate. "But the only helmet that would fit O.J. was all white, and he used it to psychological advantage. He wanted everyone to know it was O.J. Simpson coming through that line, because a lot of players would tense up when they saw him coming. And O.J. would just give a fake and flash right by them."

The four-year colleges had not ignored O.J.'s spectacular performances at City College. He accepted an athletic scholarship to the University of Southern California for two more years of varsity competition. In his first year (as a junior), O.J. gained national recognition. He rushed for 1,543 yards and led Southern Cal to a 14–3 Rose Bowl victory over Indiana. The Trojans were overwhelmingly chosen as national champions in the postseason ratings.

Simpson's supporters thought that he should have won the Heisman Trophy as the top college player in the nation. But it was a tradition that the Heisman Trophy go to seniors, and O.J. lost it. The question was whether he could turn in another season anywhere near as good.

In the very first game of his senior year, O.J. broke his own records. He gained 236 yards in 39 carries against Minnesota, caught six passes for 59 more yards and scored four touchdowns. The crucial one came midway through the fourth quarter, when the Trojans were trailing 20–16. They took possession on their 45-yard line, and then O.J. took over. Running off tackle, up the middle and around end, he carried the ball six straight times, gained the 55

In the 1967 Rose Bowl, Southern Cal's O. J. Simpson dives over the goal line.

O.J. hams it up as rival running back Franco Harris is being interviewed for television.

yards and banged over for the winning touchdown. For the season, O.J. again rushed for more than 1,500 yards.

At the end of his senior year O.J. was the all but unanimous choice for the Heisman Trophy. Then, in a nationwide poll, he was voted the greatest college running back of the past *fifty years.* Needless to say, every team in the NFL wanted him.

The team with the first draft choice was Buffalo. For O.J., Buffalo wasn't the most attractive city—he had always lived and played ball in sunny California. "What's Buffalo like?" he asked Bills owner Ralph Wilson. "My image of the town is cars stalled in a blizzard with snow piled on all the houses."

Simpson proved to be a hard bargainer. He negotiated with the Bills for eight months, hoping they would agree to trade him to a more attractive town. Then he finally signed a four-year contract that guaranteed him almost $400,-000. In addition, he signed deals with a car company, a soft-drink company and a television network to help them promote their products. Combined with his football income, these contracts made him a millionaire in his first season.

But he had still not proven himself in the NFL, and the fans in Buffalo were not all on his side after his comments about their city. Then he reported to training camp and met coach John Rauch. Rauch believed that the way to win in the NFL was with a passing attack. All through that first dismal season, he made no effort to take advantage of Simpson's skills as a ball-carrier. The coach wouldn't use O.J. as a receiver, either—he seldom sent him out of the backfield on pass routes, although O.J. had shown in college that he could catch the ball.

By the end of his rookie season Simpson had gained 697 yards on the ground and 343 on pass plays—mostly short desperation passes from a quarterback who was about to be tackled. The Bills won four games and lost ten. AFL Rookie-of-the-Year honors went to Carl Garrett of Boston, who gained fewer yards on the ground and on passes than Simpson.

"It was understandable that Garrett won," said O.J., "because people had expected great things from me, and I had fallen far short. But I didn't go into the season looking for a trophy. I

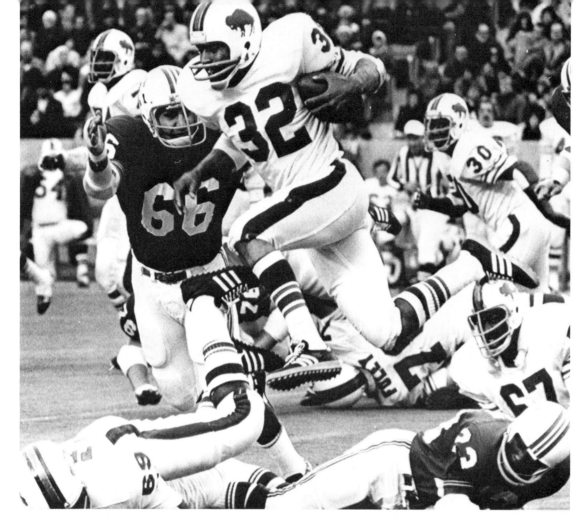

Simpson flies through the air for a big Buffalo gain against the New England Patriots.

wanted to give the people the touchdowns [he scored only two] and thrills that they expected of me. And I wanted to make the Bills into a winner. When I couldn't do those things, consolation prizes didn't matter."

Simpson's second season in Buffalo was even more frustrating. He was running well and feeling more comfortable when he injured a knee returning a kickoff. He was sidelined for the year after gaining 488 yards and scoring six touchdowns. The only good thing was that the injury did not require surgery. Before the 1971 season opened, coach Rauch was fired. Finally O.J. could talk about his frustrations.

"My first two years, they never used me right," he said, carefully avoiding the mention of Rauch's name. "They never threw the ball to me as a primary receiver, or set up any screen passes for me. And as a ball-carrier, I was always running off tackle or up the middle. I consider myself a good broken-field runner, but I was never permitted to run sweeps or run any draw plays. Running the ball up the middle was insane. You are not going to jam the ball down anybody's throat if you don't have the horses up front to block."

Buffalo's player-personnel director Harvey Johnson took over as interim coach in '71. O.J. liked Johnson, but by then the team had deteriorated and the blocking was even worse. Buffalo had the poorest record in the league. O.J. gained 742 yards for the season, but

Swarmed over by Pittsburgh tacklers, Simpson is about to go down on the muddy field.

there were rumors that he would play out his option in 1972 and try to sign up with another team.

Then Lou Saban, who had coached the Bills to championships in the early years of the AFL, returned to Buffalo as the coach for '72. Halfback Floyd Little, who had rushed for over 1,100 yards with Saban's Denver Broncos in 1971, told O.J.: "My first two years at Denver were terrible. My advice to you is to hang in there. Your day will come."

Simpson took one look at Saban's new playbook for the Bills and was happy. "His playbook was geared to the run," said O.J., who had averaged over 30 carries per game in college and less than 14 carries per game as a pro. He wanted more action and knew he would get it under Saban. "We'll have a ball-control offense like the great Packer teams had," he said, and promptly extended his contract with the Bills for four more years.

Saban brought in a lot of new players and made tremendous overall improvements in the Bills during the exhibition season. But then the Bills were struck with a succession of injuries that kept them buried in the second division. They were finally using Simpson, though. And at long last, O.J. was beginning to look like the greatest running back the colleges had turned out in 50 years. He carried 292 times, averaged an amazing 4.3 yards per rush, and led the league in rushing.

"He's just so quick," said Jet safety Gus Hollomon. "There's no way you can play the angles to tackle him. I remember one play where he was running down the sidelines and I was closing on a perfect angle to stop him. He stiff-armed me, put a finger in my eye and kept on going without stepping out of bounds. All I got out of it was a black eye. He's unbelievable."

"I'm amazed to see I'm leading the league in rushing," O.J. said late in the '72 season. "What could it be like if everyone was healthy?" he wondered.

With that hunger to be the best still gnawing at him, O.J. Simpson would find out in the years ahead.

Otis Taylor

Otis Taylor (right) hugs Mike Garrett after scoring a touchdown for Kansas City.

Kansas City Chiefs flanker Otis Taylor stood 6-foot-3, weighed 215 pounds, could run like a deer, leap like a gazelle —and catch any football thrown within five yards of his acrobatic body. Once he had caught the ball, he had the speed and moves and strength to run short gains into very long gains.

After Taylor had displayed his spectacular skills in a nationally televised game between the Chiefs and Jets, ex-quarterback Don Meredith said: "If ole Otis isn't the best receiver in the league, I don't know who is."

Perhaps the finest tribute Taylor ever received came from the great Don Hutson, who caught 100 touchdown passes for the Green Bay Packers between 1935 and 1945. Taylor met Hutson at an awards dinner following the 1971 season and, shaking his hand, said, "I've read all about you, Mr. Hutson, and you were the greatest."

"I've *seen* you play," Don said, "and you *are* the greatest."

Yet in his first seven seasons in professional football, Otis Taylor was never named All-Pro flanker. "I don't know why I haven't made All-Pro," Otis said. "It's one thing that a player, as an individual, sometimes worries about, the lack of recognition. I know I've felt overlooked from time to time, but who could I complain to?"

Hank Stram, the Chiefs' coach, couldn't understand Taylor's not making All-Pro, either, particularly after the '71 season when Otis was the only player in the league to gain over 1,000 yards on pass receptions. His 57 catches were good for 1,110 yards—which averaged out to a gain of almost 20 yards every time he hauled in a pass.

"People ask me about the year Otis had," said Stram. "I don't think he's any different than he's ever been for us, except that he's been able to stay healthy. I think when he is able to play and express his ability, there's not a better flanker—there's not a better athlete—in professional football."

The All-Pro rating may have eluded Taylor because of some nasty rumors that were spread over the years, suggesting that Otis was lazy, that he did not work to play up to his potential and that he did not try to be the very best receiver in football. Such rumors may have stuck in the minds of those who voted for the All-Pro selections.

"That's the most ridiculous thing I've ever heard," Taylor replied. "I'll tell you something about Otis Taylor. He wants to be the best—always. There hasn't been a year he played when he didn't want to score more touchdowns

Taylor makes a spectacular one-handed catch of a pass against the Buffalo Bills in 1971.

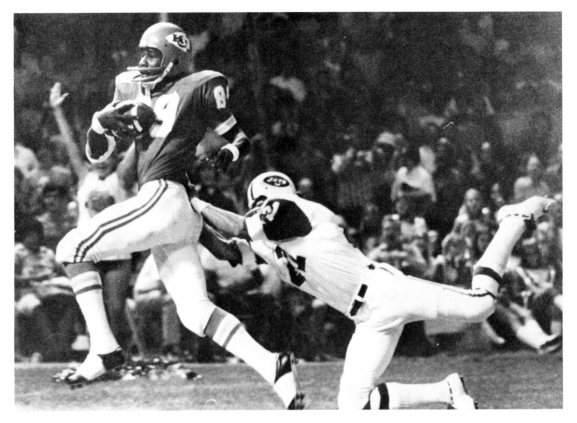

The Jets' Steven Tannen grabs at Taylor and misses as the speedy receiver steps into the end zone.

than anybody, gain more yardage than anybody.

"At the first of every season I start out aiming to be among the top ten pass receivers in the league. And I don't quit. I know every week if I'm having a good game. I know if I'm busy, if I'm catching passes, gaining yards. And I know that if I have enough good games, week after week, at the end of 14 games I'll have had the kind of season I want. Every year I start off with the same goals —I want to be the number one receiver in the NFL, and I want my team to be in another championship game."

It was true that Otis ran with a lazy-looking long stride, more like a distance runner than a sprinter. He seemed to be gliding rather than running all-out on pass routes. But he could still cover 40 yards in 4.5 seconds, which is very fast for anyone—and extremely fast for a 215-pounder. His long strides not only fooled fans, they fooled many a

defender who tried to keep up with Otis Taylor on Sunday afternoons.

Otis was born in 1942, in Houston, Texas. In high school he excelled in baseball, basketball and football. He played quarterback in high school football and won a scholarship to Prairie View A&M, a Negro college outside Houston. There he played quarterback as a freshman, but he became a wide receiver a year later.

"The coach saw me warming up, passing the ball back and forth in practice one day," Otis recalled. "He noticed how well I was catching the ball and suggested I become a flanker. We had a better quarterback in Jim Kearney [who later played defensive back with the Chiefs]. So I was lucky the coach switched me and lucky that I was at a school that played a pro-type offense."

He made the NAIA (small college) All-America team in 1964 and was drafted by the Chiefs of the American Football League and the Cowboys of the NFL. The two leagues were at war, each trying to sign the top college players. In his effort to keep Taylor for the Cowboys, a team representative hid him from the Chiefs at a motel near Dallas. But a Kansas City scout, Lloyd Wells, had known Taylor since high school and he started calling all of the girls Otis was known to have dated. One girl knew which motel Taylor was at. Wells snuck behind the motel and got Taylor's attention by knocking on his window. Then the scout made Otis a better offer than the Cowboys, so Otis jumped out the back window and "escaped" with the Chief scout. He signed with Kansas City.

Taylor immediately showed tremendous ability, but he needed lots of practice running his pass patterns. Coach Hank Stram brought him along slowly as a receiver, while making use of his size and speed on the kickoffs and punt returns.

Otis worked on his pass catching in practice every day. Veteran flanker Chris Burford was willing to offer advice, but for a long time, Otis seemed unwilling to accept it.

"I'd go out on a pass and maybe I'd mess it up," Taylor later recalled. "Chris would call me out and tell me what I'd done wrong. I was suspicious. 'Man,' I thought, 'why is this guy trying to put you down?' It seemed he was always calling me out. Finally it dawned on me what Chris was doing. 'Otis,' I thought, 'this guy is trying to *help* you.' And I began to listen to him."

It was a good thing he listened, because in a late November game Burford

suffered a shoulder separation. Taylor went in as Burford's replacement, and his performance in the season's final three games was sensational. Otis caught 26 passes for 446 yards and five touchdowns. He was so good that coach Stram soon gave up the Chiefs' other veteran wide receiver, Frank Jackson, to an expansion team. Taylor became a starter in Jackson's place the following season and caught 58 passes for 1,297 yards and eight touchdowns. And the Chiefs, who had a 7–5–2 record the previous season, won eleven games, then defeated Buffalo for the 1966 AFL championship. This put the Chiefs into the first Super Bowl, against Green Bay.

"The biggest factor in our winning the title was Otis Taylor," said veteran tight end Fred Arbanas. "He's our success story. He not only gives us the long-ball threat, he does a great job of blocking. Most flankers just like to catch the ball and don't care for hitting. But Otis doesn't mind sticking his head in there."

"Our offense used to go by bus," said Stram. "Now, with Otis, we take the jet." He was speaking of all the long gains Taylor made that season. He caught a 71-yard touchdown pass against the Bills, a 74-yarder against the Broncos, a 77-yarder against the Oilers and an 89-yarder against the Dolphins.

Taylor was so strong that he didn't even have to outrun the defenders to score long touchdowns. On the 89-yarder, he caught a short sideline pass. Darting past the cornerback covering him, Otis angled downfield on a diagonal. Two pursuers closed in on him around the 35-yard line, and Otis faked past one and bumped past the other.

Still another pair of would-be tacklers raced over and got their hands on Taylor at the 20, but he simply ran through them, shrugging them off.

In the Super Bowl, on January 15, 1967, Taylor glided free deep down the middle and caught a 31-yard pass that set up Kansas City's only touchdown. But the Chiefs lost 35–10. The Chiefs slipped to second place in their conference in 1967. In 1968, Otis missed six games with a painful muscle pull, and the Chiefs lost out again.

In 1969 the Chiefs fought their way to the top again—thanks partly to Otis Taylor. In the AFL playoff the Chiefs and Jets were tied 6–6 late in the fourth quarter. The Chiefs, having trouble moving the ball all game, were back on their 20-yard line. Suddenly Taylor ran a crossing pattern down the middle, caught quarterback Len Dawson's perfect pass and dashed to a 61-yard gain. On the next play the Chiefs scored and won the game. Once more they were headed for the Super Bowl.

In Super Bowl IV, the Chiefs were leading the Minnesota Vikings by only two points in the third quarter. Quarterback Dawson sent Taylor on a short sideline pattern to pick up a first down. Otis leaped to make the catch, pulled away from cornerback Earsell Mackbee and raced to a 46-yard touchdown that put Kansas City ahead 16–7. The Chiefs went on to win, 23–7.

In 1970 the Chiefs played poorly and Taylor was one reason, as he caught only 34 passes. The next year he bounced back with 67 receptions good for 1,110 yards, and the Chiefs bounced with him into the playoffs. By 1972, though, it was apparent that the aging

Taylor stays one step ahead of a defender.

133

Chiefs would have to do some quick rebuilding to get back into contention. Otis missed several games with injuries, yet still caught 57 passes for 821 yards and six touchdowns. But Kansas City ended up with an 8–6 record, out of the playoffs. Otis was disappointed with the team's finish, but not dejected by the fact that he hadn't caught more passes.

He felt that wide receivers would be catching fewer and fewer passes in the future. More and more teams were using zone defenses that permitted double coverage on both wide receivers. "That means running backs are going to be used more as receivers," he explained. "We now have a lot of patterns where we're just decoys for the backs coming in behind us to make the catch. In other words, we go in and clear out an area—stretch the zone out—so that

Muddy and wet, Taylor rests on the bench.

a back can then catch the pass underneath. But to decoy sometimes is the winning way, and that's the big thing I'm interested in—winning."

Otis had a reputation as a bit of a hothead in college, where he was nick-named "Slug" after he punched an op-ponent who fouled him. As a pro, he kept his temper under wraps for the most part, but occasionally it surfaced. At least once it cost the Chiefs dearly. That was in a 1970 game against arch-rival Oakland. Quarterback Len Dawson, trying to pass for a key first down, was trapped and had to run. Dawson ran very well, too, picking up the first down. But after he was on the ground, Raider defensive end Ben Davidson slammed into him. Enraged, Taylor ran over, jerked the 6-foot-8 Davidson off Dawson and slugged him. Penalties were called on both teams, so the play had to be run over. The Chiefs' touchdown drive ended, and Oakland went on to tie the game on a field goal in the closing seconds.

"I heard plenty about that," said Taylor, who lived in Kansas City with his wife Cheryl. "People kept coming up to me in my restaurant, the Flanker's Lounge, and saying, 'Don't do the same thing again. You made us lose that game.' "

Otis shook his head. "You know, I've had small kids ask me, 'Are you really a mean guy?' I'm not. I think I'm a gentle person, a person who cares about others. For example, I got a call from a lawyer today. A boy I know is doing time in jail. When he gets out, they want someone from the black community who gets along with kids to watch over that boy. I'm going to do it. I want to do it. When people have this respect for me, this faith in me, I don't brush off my responsibility as a citizen."

Paul Warfield

From the moment he entered the National Football League in 1964, Paul Warfield was known as "Mr. Unemotional." Whether he caught ten passes in a game or none at all, the sprinter-fast wide receiver would respond in the same quiet, patient way to the probing questions of reporters after the game.

Warfield even reacted calmly and coolly to what seemed like the most disastrous news of his career. In January of 1970, Art Modell, owner of the Cleveland Browns, told Warfield that he had been traded to the Miami Dolphins. Paul had been a star of the Browns for six years, and nearly every season the team was fighting for the championship. The Dolphins, on the other hand, had

Although double-teamed by Colt defenders, Paul Warfield catches a touchdown pass for Miami.

won only three games in 1969. In addition, Warfield would have to move his family from their home in Cleveland. Yet he refused to let it bother him.

"I knew I hadn't been traded because I lacked ability or because of deterioration of my ability," Paul said. "I just had to convince myself to be optimistic. When Art Modell called to tell me about the trade, he wished me luck. I wished him luck, too, and told him I knew I would be successful."

But Warfield had no idea how successful. Two years later, in January 1972, he would recall that trade after a Dolphin practice for the Super Bowl.

"A few days after that call from Modell," Paul remembered, "I was lying on the sofa half asleep when the television sports news came on. I sat up. Don Shula had been hired to coach the Dolphins. Right away I began to be more optimistic. I knew about Shula's record, and I felt he would make a winner out of Miami."

In six years as coach at Baltimore, Shula had had phenomenal success, winning 73 games. He soon proved that he could do wonders at Miami, too. Looking back after the 1971 season, Warfield said, "The way we started out in preseason a year ago, I began to think he might whip us together for an 8–6 season. Instead, we were 10–4 and made the playoffs. This year we not only made the playoffs, we won them. And now we're in the Super Bowl." The Dolphins broke all records the next season by winning 17 games in a row, including the Super Bowl.

There were two breakthrough games that were all-important in the sudden emergence of the Dolphins. Paul War-

field played a big part in both of them. The first, early in the 1970 season, was against the Oakland Raiders. In four years the Dolphins had never beaten Oakland. But then, in front of 57,140 fans in the Orange Bowl in Miami, the Dolphins won, 20–13.

Warfield caught only three passes in the game. But two of them went for touchdowns and the other—a 54-yard gainer on the slippery, rain-soaked artificial turf—set up a third Dolphin touchdown. On all three catches Warfield beat Raider cornerback Willie Brown, who Shula thought was "the best defensive back in football."

The first touchdown, which covered 49 yards, was the most spectacular. It showed Warfield's magnificent running ability after a catch. He ran a turn-in over the middle and grabbed the pass only nine yards from the line of scrimmage. Seeing running room to his right, he cut back, picked up a blocker and sped down to the Oakland 25. Three defenders converged on him there, and he seemed certain to be tackled. But Paul did a complete 360-degree spin on the wet turf and whirled away from the would-be tacklers to go in and score.

"That spin was just something I did instinctively," Paul said through a large smile afterward.

Only Shula's smile was larger in the winners' locker room. "We think Paul's the best receiver in football," the coach said. "And he went a long way toward proving it tonight in a big game."

Dolphin president Joe Robbie called it "the biggest win in our history."

In that win over Oakland, Miami proved that it could beat a top team. Then in 1971 it proved it could bounce back from a big deficit against a rugged defensive team—the Pittsburgh Steelers. Dolphin quarterback Bob Griese, who had been hospitalized the day before with food poisoning, did not start the game. The Dolphins were unable to move against the Steelers until late in

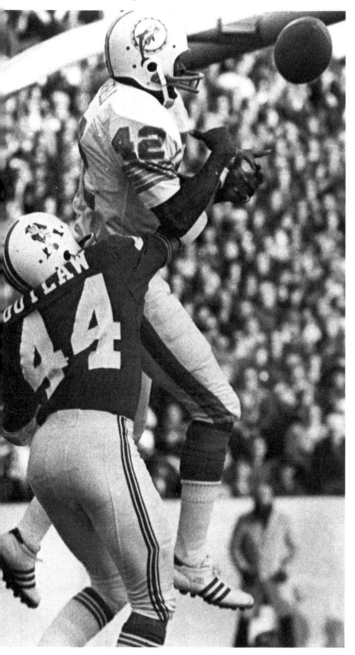

Another touchdown catch for Warfield.

the second quarter, with Pittsburgh leading 21–3.

Then Griese came in and took the Dolphins down to the Steeler 12-yard line. Warfield, who roomed with Griese in training camp, told the quarterback he thought he could get open near the goal post. Paul set out to the right, went downfield, faked to the sideline, then cut sharply toward the post between two safetymen. When Warfield's foot hit the goal line, the ball hit him in the chest: 21–10.

The next time Miami got the ball, Griese faded to pass from his 14-yard line. Warfield lost his defender and was open on a post pattern right away, but Griese was under too much pressure to see him. Bob scrambled right, left, then suddenly stopped and heaved a long pass downfield. Warfield caught it near the Steeler 40, and ran 46 more yards to score: 21–17.

"During training camp Bob and I discuss just about every situation that can come up," Paul said later. "When I looked back and saw him scrambling, I started to cut to my right—the direction he was running. Then I saw him reverse his field and out of the corner of my eye I saw the defensive back who was covering me move toward the line to stop a run. So I just turned downfield and Bob was looking for my move."

On the first play of the fourth quarter Warfield scored what proved to be the winning touchdown. He ran a simple fly pattern, straight down the sideline, got a step ahead of the cornerback and caught Griese's perfectly arched pass over his shoulder. The defender dove at Warfield's legs, missed, and Paul trotted into the end zone: 24–21.

137

Cool, calm Paul Warfield.

Dolphin tight end Marv Fleming compared Warfield to other great receivers: "Sure catcher—Carroll Dale was the only one in the league in a class with Paul. Moves—no one was in Warfield's class. Not just speed, he has *control* of that speed—acceleration and deceleration. Charley Taylor was the only receiver in the NFL who could control his speed like Paul. He's cool and calm—the one you can count on."

"I thought I knew Warfield when he was with the Browns," said Shula. "But you get additional respect for him by finding out what makes him tick. He's a leader, quiet, but there's something about the way he carries himself. You look up to him. There are things you can't measure."

"He's the only man I ever saw putting on moves when he's just walking," said George Mira, a reserve quarterback with the Dolphins in 1970.

"I guess Mira got that from training camp," Paul explained, smiling. "Sometimes when I'm walking along I think about the kind of moves I'm going to make, and I try them unconsciously."

Warfield began working on his moves at the First Street Grammar School in Warren, Ohio, where there was a touch-football league for youngsters. A 72-pounder, he was a very tricky end even then. But when he got to junior high school, he wasn't allowed to go out for the tackle team.

"I weighed only 95 pounds," Paul recalled, "and my mother was afraid I'd be run over. She said nothing doing. So I stayed away and delivered newspapers."

Fortunately, Paul's father, who had played football himself, wanted to see his son play in high school. The Warren High team was the big topic of conversation at the Republic Steel plant where his dad worked. When Paul was a freshman, his weight was up to 130 and his dad allowed him to go out for football. Although he had never played tackle football before, Paul not only made the team but became a star as a shifty, speedy running back.

Nearly 70 colleges offered Paul football scholarships. Two Ohio State grads who lived in Warren convinced Paul that he should become a Buckeye, and

Warfield shows another athletic talent, breaking the tape for Ohio State in the low hurdles.

he did. After all, he was a running back, and Ohio State was famous for its running game. The problem, as it turned out, was that Ohio State coach Woody Hayes liked power football—he had his fullback carry the ball on nearly every play. Warfield was a halfback, and Hayes just wasn't interested in a break-

away runner. But Paul managed to make the All–Big Ten team two years, due mainly to his fine blocking ability. Everyone agreed that even if he didn't run very often, he was a big threat.

"I saw him play three times," said Cleveland Browns' player-personnel director Paul Bixler. "And in those games he didn't have a chance to do anything outstanding. But I could see the opposition was scared to death of him. They always seemed afraid he'd break away for the long one. Several times he got behind the defense on pass routes, but he rarely was thrown the ball."

The Browns were impressed enough to make Warfield their first draft choice. They considered him a top candidate as a defensive back. "But when we took one look at his moves in camp," said Bixler, "there was only one position for him. He was the answer to one of our real needs—flanker."

Warfield had also been drafted by the Buffalo Bills of the AFL, and they offered the same $15,000 salary and $5,000 bonus as Cleveland. But Paul had another problem. At Ohio State he had become a track star and he had dreams of competing in the 1964 Olympics. A long-jumper, he had leaped 26 feet, 2 inches in one meet against the Russians and had a good shot at qualifying for the U.S. team. But the Browns and Bills warned that they couldn't guarantee their offers if he got hurt in track. Paul finally decided to forget the Olympics and sign with Cleveland.

"There was the possibility that a year out of football—which was what it would have amounted to if I'd made the Olympics—would have been a serious handicap to me," Paul said later. "If I had to do it all over again, I'd still go into the pros immediately after college. I had to do what I thought was best for Paul Warfield in the long run. I think I did that."

Certainly the Browns thought so, as Warfield made the Pro Bowl squad his very first season, catching 52 passes for 920 yards and nine touchdowns. He went on to make All-Pro in three of his six seasons with them (he missed one full season because of injuries). The Browns only traded him because they desperately needed a top young quarterback. In exchange for Warfield they got a first-round draft choice and drafted Mike Phipps.

The Dolphins did well on the trade, too. With Warfield's help, they made the playoffs his first year and made the Super Bowl in 1971. In 1972, Paul had another great season, averaging 20.9 yards per reception as the Dolphins went undefeated from opening day to the Super Bowl.

Facing Washington in Super Bowl VII, Warfield made three important catches for 36 yards and two important first downs. He also made a long touchdown catch that was called back because of a penalty.

But great receivers can contribute even when they aren't catching passes. Early in the Super Bowl game, the Dolphins' other wide receiver, Howard Twilley, caught a touchdown pass. One big reason—the Redskins were using double coverage on Paul Warfield, leaving only one defender for Twilley. The Dolphins won 14–7.

"I guess we've proved to all our critics that we're the number one team in football," Paul said after the game. It was a strong statement from "Mr. Unemotional." But it was spoken in the emotion-charged Dolphin dressing room after they had become world champions . . . and even Paul Warfield had to get caught up in that glorious atmosphere.

Gene Washington

Quarterback John Brodie got the headlines when he brought the 49ers from a 17–6 deficit to a 20–17 victory over the Vikings in the final game of the 1972 season. He entered the game with only nine minutes remaining, after being sidelined most of the season. But it was wide receiver Gene Washington who made the most spectacular play in the comeback that clinched the NFC Western Division title for the 49ers.

Brodie, his arm rusty from inactivity, threw his first long pass well wide of Washington. Somehow, though, Gene leaped and stretched and finger-tipped the ball. He came down with it while

keeping his balance, then put on some beautiful broken-field running moves and sped 53 yards through the Vikings for the touchdown.

And on the winning touchdown pass, it was Washington who tied up not two but *three* Minnesota defenders and thus allowed another receiver, Dick Witcher, to get open for the catch. Of course, Gene Washington had been performing such heroics all season. The touchdown catch was his twelfth of the season, giving him the league lead. And he averaged 20 yards gained on each of his 46 receptions. He made All-Pro for the second time and was named to the Pro Bowl squad for the third time in his four seasons in the NFL.

"I want success and I'll get it," Washington once said. "I set high goals and I go for them."

Which only made one wonder just what other goals he might be after.

Gene Washington grew up in Long Beach, California, where his father provided very well for his wife and five sons by working as an industrial painter in the Naval Shipyard. Gene and his four brothers were outstanding athletes who all eventually earned athletic scholarships to college. Gene's parents appreciated the boys' athletic ability as long as they kept scholarship first and athletics second. According to the Washingtons, education was the way to get ahead in this world—and who wanted to be behind?

At Polytechnical High School, Gene made all-city in both basketball and football. But that wasn't all. He also achieved a 3.6 (or A-minus) grade average. And in his senior year, the young black athlete was elected student body president of the predominantly white school.

"The basketball coach interested me in running as president of the sophomore class," recalled Gene. "I lost, but I didn't like the idea of losing, so I ran for junior class president. I made a good speech and I had a good grade average, but I lost again. In my senior year I was captain of the football and basketball teams and I made a strong campaign for president of the student body. I won."

His desire to excel was just as strong on the football field. A quarterback, he passed for over 1,100 yards as a senior. With his athletic talent, academic ability and extracurricular successes, Gene was sought out by many top colleges. He received more than 50 offers to such outstanding institutions of learning as UCLA, USC, Yale, Harvard, Michigan and Stanford.

"All my orientation until that time had been toward getting into the mainstream of white society, of being successful," Gene said. "Stanford offered those possibilities more than any other school. It was a good school academically and it looked upon its ballplayers as both students and athletes."

As a running quarterback, Gene seemed to have little potential for pro ball and wasn't even considering football as a possible career. He performed well as a member of the undefeated freshman team, then played only sporadically as a sophomore. Then he began to consider the money and prestige that came to college stars who turned pro. He began to think that he ought to take a shot at the NFL. This caused him to reevaluate his skills.

One that got away: the ball slips through Washington's hands as he falls over Atlanta's Ken Reaves.

"I felt I didn't have a pro arm to make it as a quarterback," he said later, "and I also felt there was a prejudice against black quarterbacks in the NFL."

So just before his junior year at Stanford, Washington went to coach John Ralston and asked to be moved from quarterback to end. Gene had shown so much speed and quickness that Ralston thought the change was a good idea.

The switch wasn't hard for Gene, since he had already had some practice. "When you spend at least an hour a day throwing a football," he said, "someone has to throw it back and you have to catch it. That and the fact that I had played basketball helped my timing and use of my hands."

He became a starter immediately, and as a junior caught 48 passes for 575 yards. The next year, sophomore Jim Plunkett became the varsity quarterback, and he and Washington combined to break a number of Stanford records. Gene had 13 receptions in one game, three touchdown catches in another. For the season he caught 71 passes and gained 1,117 yards.

He didn't neglect his studies, either. A sociology major, Gene maintained a B average and as a senior even put his sociology to practical use. He was a co-founder of Interact, an integrated student organization "designed to promote contact and understanding between Stanford students and minority groups living in ghetto areas near the campus."

"The problem that most young people from that area face," said Gene, "is motivation to stay in school. It was a little easier for me because my parents were always pretty sticky about me doing well in school."

San Francisco 49er quarterback John Brodie knew Washington would do well when he finished school, too. "Washington will be a number one draft choice in the pros," Brodie told the 49ers. "He's a natural receiver. Gene has moves you can't teach."

Brodie was a Stanford graduate who helped coach the team in spring practice. He had worked closely with Gene when he was still a quarterback and had passed to him during workouts after the youngster became a receiver.

Not surprisingly, Gene Washington

Washington snags the ball on an 86-yard touchdown play against the Redskins.

was the 49ers' first draft pick in 1969. In his first season he caught 51 passes for 711 yards and three touchdowns. The next year he increased his reception total to 53, and his yardage zoomed to 1,100. He was a unanimous All-Pro selection.

"He catches anything thrown near him, and he can go pretty good with the ball after he gets it," said Brodie, who admired Washington so much that the two became roommates on 49er road trips. "If Gene has a weakness," John continued, "I don't know what it is. And that goes for him as a man as well as a player."

Brodie was white, twelve years older than Washington and a very successful businessman in the offseason. This would seem to give him an entirely different perspective than his young receiver. Quite the contrary, said John: "We think alike."

"Washington is just not an average end in the National Football League," said 49er coach Dick Nolan. "As a rookie he was far ahead of the average first-year man, and he increased the distance between him and the other receivers from year to year. He now has the knowledge of a guy a lot more experienced. He's got great poise, strength and a lot of moxie.

"He can do things that other wide receivers can't do, no matter how experienced they are. You just don't bump him at the line of scrimmage and forget him. Jerry LeVias is a fine receiver, for example, but when he was with Houston they had to put him in motion before the snap to get him open. He couldn't fight the backs to get downfield. But Gene has the strength to get open, and once he catches the ball he can really move."

Washington stood 6-foot-1 and weighed 188 pounds. He looked almost skinny on the field—until a defensive back tried to bump him and tie him up at the line of scrimmage. To the dismay of the defender, Gene would run right through the bump and be downfield before the cornerback could recover. There was a lot of sinewy muscle be-

neath Washington's slight-looking frame.

Surprisingly, though, he was a poor blocker his first season as a pro. "Blocking, like pass catching," said 49er end coach Jim Shofner, "is kind of an art. Not everybody can do it. It took Gene time to learn, but he sure can block now."

"Our receivers did not do a whole lot of blocking in my rookie year," said Gene. "So the next year at training camp in Santa Barbara, the coaches got us on the two-man blocking sled every day, just like linemen. No one had ever shown me how to block before. Here I was in my second year of pro football, just learning how to block for the first time. Our line coach, Ernie Zwahlen, just kept working us on the fundamentals.

"I didn't like it much at first," Gene continued. "Hell, I didn't especially want to go down there and hit those guys. I wanted to catch passes. But all of a sudden it got to be fun. I got a good feeling knocking a guy down and knowing that I was helping the team. Now any time I get a chance to go after a defensive man, I do it."

In his third season in the league, 1971, Washington had to face a problem brought on by his success—double coverage. Almost every time he went out for a pass, he found himself guarded by two defenders instead of one. Gene still managed to pick up tremendous yardage with every catch—averaging 19.2 yards per reception—but his total receptions fell to 46.

"The double-coverage is frustrating," said Gene, "because I like to catch the ball like everyone else. But when they're doubling on me, I know someone else

On his way into the end zone—Gene Washington scores again for San Francisco.

is getting open, so it helps the team."

"If I were playing against Gene, I would push him or hold him," said assistant coach Jim Shofner, a former NFL defensive back. "There just isn't any legal way that one man can stop him. He has to be double-teamed."

The Thanksgiving game of 1972 between the 49ers and Cowboys showed just how valuable Gene Washington was. Both teams felt they had to win if they were going to make the post-season playoffs. Through most of the first half the Cowboys totally dominated the 49ers, who simply couldn't move on offense. Then the 49er defense ran back a Dallas fumble for a touchdown to tie the score, 7–7. This seemed to pick up the offense, and suddenly the line blocking was a little crisper, and quarterback Steve Spurrier, replacing the injured Brodie, got a split second more time to pass.

Washington told Spurrier in the huddle that he could get open for a short pass over the middle, before the safety-man could get up to aid the cornerback covering him. The 49ers needed six yards for a first down. Washington burst straight ahead seven yards, faked to the outside, then cut sharply over the middle as the ball arrived. First down.

Two plays later Gene told Spurrier he thought he could go all the way—some 50 yards—for a touchdown pass. Gene had been running so many short pat-terns that he thought the Cowboys wouldn't expect him to go deep. He was right. Gene dashed past cornerback Charlie Waters, faked toward the sideline when he reached safety Cliff Harris, then burst toward the goal post all alone. The long pass hung in the air, and just as Gene jumped for it at the goal line, Waters finally caught up and ran Gene down. Interference was called, and the 49ers scored on the play after the penalty. They went on to win the game.

"The overall goal is for the team to do well," Gene said afterward. "Individual things come after that."

Off the field Gene Washington also did well. After he joined the 49ers, he helped his parents renovate their home and married beautiful model Cynthia Watson. He invested his bonus money in two successful enterprises—an insurance agency and an industrial supply firm. But Washington still wasn't satisfied.

"Although there's a lot of money to be made from my businesses, somehow they just don't turn me on," he said. "I want something else. I want to relate to the black community. There is a need for lawyers and other professional people. I want to contribute. There will be a chance for those who are prepared. I plan to be."

Based on Gene Washington's past performance, one could safely bet that he would accomplish his ultimate goals.

Index

149

150